# EIGHT WHEELS

## PREFACE

*Iraq 1968, prior to the coming of Saddam Hussein at the time when Hassan the dictator was in situ. We had arrived at an Army checkpoint, two vehicles that had unwittingly missed the border check point. A Captain, who we discovered spoke amazingly good English walked over towards us as we were forced to stop by several concrete filled oil drums along the very dusty road. Armed guards were all around us but no other vehicles, like some scene out of a movie. The Captain asked for our passports and after a brief glance informed us that in fact we had actually missed the border post which was way back in the direction from which we had come, a surprise to us all as there had been no indication along our route. The Captain very kindly offered the services of one of his soldiers to accompany us to the village where the border control was in order that we could get our passports properly stamped .*

*Travelling back along the long sandy roads which were sprayed with crude oil to avoid the sand blowing about, we eventually arrived at the missed village where the border control office was. A gentleman came out to us dressed casually, I would think in his mid forties. The Army guide explained to him in Arabic what had occurred and all hell let loose. At this point Menai and I and all of our fellow travellers had left our vehicles and were completely bemused by what was happening around us. The man ranted and raved at us in very good English, threatened us with imprisonment and ordered one of the guards to cock his automatic weapon which was poked into my back with some force. To say I was terrified was an understatement, the sweat pouring down my back, adrenalin pumping, heart racing and in that moment as he removed the gun from my back and stood to one side of me, for some bizarre reason all I could focus on was the fact that his weapon was stamped 'made in Czechoslovakia.' Drifting back to reality the man seemed to just rattle on and on for what seemed like an eternity and equally bizarrely just vanish with all our passports!*

*After a considerable and tense period, when no one dared speak or hardly dare breathe for that matter, the official re-emerged and simply said 'you are very lucky, you can go.' We were all in a state of high anxiety. No one was talking, no eye to eye contact, we just sauntered back to our vehicles afraid to be seen to be rushing when in fact we wanted to run, all of us, run for our lives. I knew that. As we left the border control post the man was still ranting, obviously someone higher in authority had overruled him and he was none too pleased. For ourselves the sense of relief was overwhelming our hearts still pounding with the thought of what had just passed.*

*Acknowledgements*

*With acknowledgements to all ten passengers who travelled with Menai and I over land to South Africa. We could not have achieved the journey without them. Unfortunately I do not remember all of their names now, many moons have passed since but they know who they are and they have always had our appreciation. With special thanks to them and also to Menai for supporting me under what was at times, very difficult circumstances.*

*A special thank you also to Michelle, my partner and friend who encouraged me to tell this story and for her help in putting it all together.*

*Dedication*


*In memory of Menai, I dedicate this book to her, our son and his family*

# Chapter One

No money as such, no suitable vehicles as such, no experience as such, why would we not contemplate a 12,000 ish mile journey over land to somewhere in the far distance, Durban, South Africa; not Australia, not New Zealand, not Canada, far too partisan, far too normal. I wanted to do something different I needed the challenge and Menai, by then my wife, came along for the ride and indulged me.

Of course we were not the first, nor would be the last people to drive over land to South Africa. In fact whilst we were making our plans we came into contact with two other men from London who were also planning a trip overland, taking ten people straight across Africa north to south via Egypt, Sudan and the Congo. They had acquired we understood, two long wheeled based Series 1 'Land Rovers, 1950's vintage, which they had apparently overhauled. We were to hear about their personal adventure after reaching South Africa, suffice to say things did not work out as they expected. In fact during our journey, we also met up with a lecturer in Nairobi who told us that many years before, he had also driven to South Africa in an Austin 7 across the Sahara. He said it had been unbelievable really, so perhaps our efforts were not unique, but we were unique and we hoped our experiences as individuals would be.

At the climax of our journey and once we had settled in South Africa, we met up with a Dutch couple who lived in Johannesburg, they told us about two of their relatives who had driven back in a Land Rover overland and in Southern Egypt had their vehicle impounded by rogue elements of the Egyptian Army, which necessitated their two relatives having to make their own way back, without vehicle, all the way back to Holland!

Just after the Second World War it was not unusual for demobbed soldiers to drive overland to South Africa in ex-Army vehicles so in essence and historically travelling across Africa by whatever means was wholly acceptable or should I say commonplace despite the terrain and politics of the area.

I was twenty three years old. Durban's history, the struggles of its inhabitants were never in my mind, just a desire to escape from the mundane and to resurrect myself elsewhere and Durban just happened to be it.

Durban. One of the largest cities on the Indian Ocean, historically, the Drakensberg mountains inhabited by hunter-gatherers since 100,000 BC. Vasco de Gama, the famous sea dog arrived there in the year 1497 and in 1835, the town was named Durban after the Cape Governor Benjamin D'Urban. Today Durban is inhabited by a mixture of Black Africans, Indian/Asian, White and others; languages encompassing English, Zulu, and Afrikaans amongst many others.

Back in the 1960's South Africa was ruled by white supremacists. Racially mixed marriages were prohibited and for the Afrikaners their churches found theological reasons for apartheid. The Government enforced every Black African worker to carry a pass which was really an internal passport. Interestingly, the British first introduced this system during the Boer War. Today Durban is the largest city in the South African province of KwaZulu-Natal, the second most important manufacturing hub after Johannesburg; renowned as the busiest port in South Africa with a sub-tropical climate and extensive beaches, but it was in the 1960's where my story begins.

I had always had a desire to travel to move on, such was my restless personality. University had not lived up to its expectations wrongly or rightly. An ill chosen course perhaps, but I had never really settled in there despite my initial enthusiasm. I had something to prove, did then and do now in all honesty, even now at seventy something years of age. Back then I wanted to do something 'irrational.' My partner Menai had not been so impressed with my great idea but had 'gone along' with my plans out of love I presume but it was a big give. We moved in together, our marriage a mostly last minute affair, two witnesses, a civil ceremony lasting probably all of twenty minutes and it was all done. No music, hymns, flowers, fanfare, just a very practical step forward. I finished University without the famous degree, disappointed I was not quite as clever as I thought I was and somewhat humiliated but then was just focussed on the next challenge 'escape!' The fact that Menai was prepared to give everything up to do this with me was quite a commitment and in hindsight I think I did not appreciate how difficult it must have been at times, but that is love for you.

Firstly, the two big questions in my quest to decamp, a) by what means would we get to Durban; getting some transport cheaply would be a challenge and b) how were we going to finance the dream, as at that point it was just that. After lots of talk and arguments and decision making, the way forward was obvious to us both, we would have to take other people with us, travellers themselves, and people with their own dreams perhaps and some cash to spare. So we set about advertising and lo and behold a dozen people came forward, paid up front £130.00 all in; which at the time was quite a sum of money. Our fellow travellers were from all walks of life from all over the country and elsewhere; a doctor from Northern Ireland, a traveller from Australia, a solicitor, a mechanic, ex Air Force and a girl from the US who was travelling the world. The age range of our travellers was 20- 40, we had not asked for references. In those days of course, without the aid of the perfunctory mobile or email, all communication was by letter and landline so subsequently the whole process took quite some time. Without their financial input we had no starting point. What savings we had we just 'put in the pot' and moved on to Phase Two, the transport.

With only Michelin maps to study I began to research what vehicles we would need and more importantly could afford. In hindsight, of course and what would have been ideal for the journey would have been two second hand Land Rover Defenders. In fact some would have said essential, but in my world that was never going to happen, we simply did not have the money. Second best or perhaps seventh best in reality, revealed themselves as a Volkswagen Caravanette which we purchased privately and a Ford Transit minibus which we found in a showroom in one of the darker corners of London. I remember seeing two ambulances from Israel for sale in the same showroom, nestled cosily up to the minibus and I hoped and prayed we would never have need of one of those en route! The combi caravanette was two shades of green, handy camouflage perhaps, with a fold up bed that became a seat and a stove. The Transit had a roof rack and a dozen seats inside. With vehicles at the ready and a date arranged to meet up with our fellow travellers at a Railway Station in

London, a place that seemed to suit all concerned, we began to organise the packing and make a start.

Chaos reigned. Anticipating what we might or might not need for the next however many months, was a nightmare as I remember. A couple or three tents essential, tick, sleeping bags etc. tick. The caravanette had a combi cooker on board so all basic cooking itinery required, tick, including metal plates and cups. We bought tow rope, jerry cans, different colours of course, one for petrol, one for water. As regards the tents themselves we had no idea what tents would be the easiest to transport and in the end decided on two blow up tents and one ridge tent, a spontaneous purchase as most things were ! I did also purchase two ex-Army petrol cooking stoves, though on testing them out later one quite dramatically burst into flames! We decided against taking them, enough said.

We assumed everyone else would be equally engaged in their own packing, some a little more experienced than ourselves, some with plenty of experience and everything you could ever need in one well-worn ruck sack! Menai and I had the very necessary yellow fever jabs, which I recall rendered me incapacitated for days, though she had no reactions at all. So with passports in hand, cash in hand for fuel, we were finally ready. It was not that we were expecting to have a better life in South Africa, but a different life.

Menai had obtained a teaching position in Durban prior to our leaving and I had been interviewed by the Anglo American Corporation, which was the biggest gold mining corporation in the world at the time for a position in South Africa. I was offered a job in HR at their head office in Johannesburg and was asked to call in to their offices to firm up the position when we arrived. I was given an official letter regarding the job offer as was Menai for her teaching position and the Immigration Authorities in South Africa, as we were later to discover, were satisfied with both these letters, despite the jobs being in two completely different localities!

At the point of our leaving Menai and I were renting a flat in Watford and as a Manchester boy born and bred, having moved to London, I wanted to fly my wings, I was ready for action. There were no fears, no doubts, not a whiff of anxiety as I recall, believe that if you will. Off into the blue yonder whatever the circumstances seemed extremely appealing, I was literally raring to go.

We had met up with all of our fellow travellers at our flat in Watford several weeks before we actually 'set sail' as it were. As I remember it was all very convivial, we sat and discussed the travelling plans, the route I had in mind over a few beers and everyone appeared happy with the arrangements. The quiet before the storm as they say. Twenty three years old and with very little experience of the world we were about to set off on our journey.

On our leaving day, having given notice on our rented flat some weeks previously, Menai and I set off from the comforting drizzle and soft grey skies of England on a road to somewhere. With only £1,400 in savings for the whole journey, just a drop in the ocean by today's standards and with hindsight totally unrealistic.

On our journey to one of the tube stations in London, Cockfosters as I recall as   it seemed the most convenient to most of our fellow travellers, Menai and I were suddenly feeling strangely apprehensive about meeting up with everyone again,  but I was on a mission and I was determined I would make it all come together. We had bought a pile of pre-packaged dried foods and rice to keep us going on our journey, as back up and of course the obligatory large box of biscuits.   In hindsight it seemed incredulous that the purchase of a large cardboard box of chocolate chip cookies was uppermost on our minds, when we were about to travel across Africa in tremendous heat and humidity!  I can only imagine our brains were elsewhere at the time?

Having met up with our fellow travellers briefly and got sort of acquainted for a second time, everyone seemed to get on well at the start and so we began our long journey. Eight in the minibus and four in the caravanette and a roof rack for the luggage. There were three women travellers, the rest men, everyone just found a seat, sat back. Menai and I breathed a huge sigh of relief at the prospect of finally starting on our journey and so we began the trek.

# Chapter Two

Our journey as you might imagine, started with the ferry from the always very busy port of Dover to Calais, which was short and unremarkable, I remember all of us just being preoccupied with our thoughts of what was to come. A calm sail on a quiet day, drifting clouds above us and the usual plethora of seagulls accompanying us on the swift traverse. We were all anxious to move on into Europe, speculating about the roads ahead. Conversation flowed easily but underneath quite noticeably I believed, an element of disquiet.

On arrival at Calais we disembarked and drove on through France via the privately owned auto routes that existed at the time, very straight linear stretches of concrete, toll roads which of course you had to pay to drive on as you do now. We crossed into Germany where there were no issues with tolls and from there into Austria. Finally we drove into what was then Yugoslavia.

Along this stretch of our journey we stayed at various campsites, usually recommended to us by locals, nothing pre booked of course, all very random but serving a purpose. As we were travelling through Austria, the valves in the Volkswagen engine decided most annoyingly to disintegrate on us. We continued to chug up the Austrian hills very slowly as you might imagine and coasted down to the Yugoslavian border. I will not forget that sinking feeling in my chest and the disconcerted looks from our fellow travellers as we got out of our vehicles.

As a communist country no garage had spares and several of us were forced to take the minibus back into Germany to purchase a replacement engine. Nothing was ever very easy and the fates set to test us as at every turn it seemed. Customs did not understand why we wanted to bring a replacement engine back into Yugoslavia and so the state owned garage in Ljubljana had to write a letter in Serbo-Croat to explain we needed to replace the engine. Fortunately the garage was not too far away from Germany and eventually we were allowed to bring it along and have a re fit at the cost of £4.00, yes only £4.00, unbelievable! Once again and with hindsight, that wonderful thing that evaded me frequently should have made me see that it would have been faster to resolve the issue if we had bought the new engine in Austria. A little more expensive perhaps, but money would have been saved on the fuel, not to mention the effort in travelling back to Germany for the sake of about £10.00! All very disappointing given we had literally only just started out on our journey. However as a group we were making decisions together and finally the job was done and we were on our way again.

We heard that there had been an earthquake in Sarajevo two months previous to our travelling through there and as we drove through, I remember seeing piles of rubble, homes without windows, collapsed walls and general devastation despite the quake's relatively small magnitude. It was a sorry sight to pass through.

On route through the rest of Yugoslavia, we camped out at a farm where the farmer brewed his own plum brandy. He told us that every Friday night the local lads got together, had a meal together and inevitably they usually ended up fighting, intoxicated of course with the farmer's brandy! Whilst we were camping there we experienced this spectacle ourselves first hand and in fact Nick, our Australian traveller and a couple of others ended up bandaging the wounded at the end of the night! It was powerful stuff. Packing up the next morning, we left them all behind with their hangovers and headed off to Greece.

Pre booking campsites had not been in our remit on this journey, was this ever a good idea? To all intents and purposes we just made it up as we were going along, we had tents, three in all and sleeping bags, plenty of bottled water and as group we just cooked together. Cooking was basic, but it was edible and we survived. It was a somewhat cosy arrangement and not for everyone I would imagine.

Days travelling were long, hot and sticky for a lot of the time and after dinner we all just slept, too tired for anything else. Someone asked me some time after our journey had ended how we entertained ourselves at the end of each day, what we did to relax, game of cards maybe, bit of music, a good book? The reality and the truth of the matter was that we were just too exhausted for anything but supper and sleep. The journey so far had been a means to an end, just getting through each day, hopefully without incident. The only distraction in an evening I remember was to turn on the BBC World Service on the radio and catch up on the news!

En route to Turkey we had asked directions from the Thessalonica Police and instead of just pointing us in the right direction, a policeman on a motorcycle escorted us to the main highway and onto the border, over and above our expectations!

At the Turkish border and much to our dismay there were no two ways about it the authorities would not allow us in.

We were all perplexed, frustrated and more than just a little irritated, all for the want of a customs bond, a 'carnet de passage' in fact. This was an insurance document issued by the AA/RAC and something we had just never looked into or given any thought to. Another important something we had missed off our check list and completely overlooked. After a lot of pleading and discussion with the authorities and lengthy explanations which were pitiful in hindsight, they finally allowed us in and we were all relieved to carry on our journey to Istanbul.

Having argued with the authorities, the Turkish Motor Club eventually organised our 'carnet de passage,' not without the fortuitous help of one our travellers who just happened to be the son of a renowned banker, who kindly got in touch with the Auto Club and by some twist of fate and for a payment of £32.00 our application was accepted. Of course all this discourse took several days and we stayed in a campsite until we finally got everything sorted.

Our first visions of Istanbul were posters everywhere of General Ataturk, founder of the modern Turkey, everywhere you looked on every street corner. At the time the city as I remember looked quite dilapidated, Dolmus taxis everywhere, taxis which were in fact mini buses that could take you anywhere for just a small amount of money. It was noisy, very hot and activity everywhere. Istanbul struck me very much as a city in limbo, poverty and wealth incongruous neighbours as you travelled on through its arid landscape with very little in the way of forestation. Some people dressed traditionally in Muslim style clothing and others obviously not, adopting a more European presentation.

We eventually arrived at a campsite owned bizarrely by B.P. It was a very cheap but clean campsite, fenced off with barbed wire and in fact had a washing and ironing service as I recall, most unexpected. We set up camp, paid the fee and settled in for a few days.

Whether it be lack of insight or plain common sense I now admit, I would not allow our fellow travellers to store their luggage in the minibus, thinking only that it would ruin the seats not realising how vulnerable that left us in terms of security, luggage wise and so the inevitable happened whilst on the campsite. A great number of articles from our luggage were stolen, despite there being an armed guard in situ. Fortunately we all still had our passports but I had learned a valuable lesson at that point, John needed to think outside the box. Barbed wire fences and 24 hour guards not in place for no reason, perhaps an inside job? We would never know.

As a group and at the start of our journey I had thought I had the respect of my fellow travellers. As time went on I realised later and with hindsight (a word which I will mention numerous times in my story) that my dogged determination to do everything my way despite my huge lack of experience was beginning to alienate me. Constantly harassing my fellow travellers caused friction but I was too young and too proud to admit it. The plain fact was that I had taken on a mammoth project and despite Menai's support, it was proving extremely hard work and I would quote at this point that old adage, poor planning produces p*** poor performance.

As a group we did very little sightseeing in Istanbul, but I recall there were an abundance of restaurants, the owners of which were eager to entice you in to some less than average establishments overly keen and pushy in the extreme and the kitchens  not the most hygienic as I remember! No risk assessments or Health and Safety rules and regulations in those days. You would choose your dishes, the food was simple and heavily spiced but very cheap at the time. Interestingly and despite our anxieties none of us had any ill effects at all!

We stayed in Istanbul for just a few days and only a few days because we had to obtain Visas for Iraq from the Embassy in Ankara.

# Chapter Three

Following our escapades on route to Istanbul we travelled across the Bosphorus via a car ferry, the Bosphorus being a strait and a significant waterway between Europe and Asia, also connecting the Black Sea to the Mediterranean. It separated Turkey in Asia and Turkey in Europe and it was from there we made our way to Ankara.

Unfortunately, on reaching Ankara we could not find anywhere to camp, which was extremely frustrating as we were tired and weary after driving across the hills. We just needed to rest. Someone we asked suggested to us that we could try the National Sports Stadium for some peculiar reason, a stadium which was sited right next to the Police Station. So we decided to have a look and see. We asked at the Station and we were told we could camp outside on the grass or sleep in the bunk room in the Police station, a room the officers used for shifts. One look at this room which was to be quite blunt just filthy, our minds were made up. We politely refused and set up camp outside. The detectives spoke good English and one of them took two of our travellers into the Red Light district not so far away, ' will cost you nothing,' they said. We never knew whether it did or did not, that information remained forever their secret. We camped there for a couple of days during which time we obtained our visas for Iraq and then we continued to make our way over the mountains to Iran, at which time the Shah of Persia was still in charge.

The roads over the mountains were treacherous, grit roads some above the clouds. Mount Ararat was visible but not the Ark! Thankfully none of us at this point had succumbed to illness or sickness and we took things very slowly over a couple of days until finally, with relief we arrived at the Iranian border. Not for the faint hearted, our journey had had its moments so far. Showers were a thing of the past. In fact we were lucky to have a cat wash most days, jerry cans of water on board, toilets if not on the campsite just available fields, but we were young and such luxuries seemed irrelevant at the time. Just three tents, two blow up tents and one conventional ridge tent were all we needed on our journey. Menai and I slept in the combi caravanette which afforded a little privacy but otherwise we just made it up as we went along.

Travelling through the Iranian border was uneventful as I recall but one thing I do remember passing through the small villages of Iran, the over excitement of the inhabitants as we drove by, shouting out in Farsi, especially if one of the vehicles stopped i.e. at a road junction, the villagers would all gather round, to the extent where it was almost overwhelming and the desire to leave as soon possible equally as overwhelming. We were unsure whether it was excitement or agitation we never stopped long enough to find out.

The next leg of our journey was to locate the Iraq border. We were following a map but somehow took the wrong route and ended up at a big castle on top of a mountain. An Army officer came out to meet us. He spoke very good English and in strong terms explained we had come the wrong way! He told us that if we ventured any further, we would be in Kurdistan and would most likely be shot by the Kurds!! We were mortified.

Back down the mountain we went with extreme speed and retraced our steps. Eventually we arrived at the town of Kermanshah on the border with Iraq. Kermanshah is 525 kilometres from Tehran in the western part of Iran and its inhabitants mostly Kurdish speaking. Overnight we camped in a field which was dangerous because of bandits, but we had done this before. Fortunately all was okay that night, we had sufficient supplies food etc. which we had bought along the way, very basic but enough and mostly we cooked for ourselves.

The following morning we went through the border which ended up being a hugely long winded process.

The upshot of which was that we had to buy third party insurance to cover us for twenty eight days road travel in Iraq. All the documents were in Arabic, so we actually had no idea what was written on them.

Menai had been writing home regarding our progress on the journey as there was no other means of communication at the time and as far as I can remember no one ever spoke of being home sick .Tension sometimes reared its head in the group and was always concerned the frequent and disorganised mess we found ourselves in at every peak and turn. Our fellow travellers seemed disgruntled and frustrated on occasions,  but on the whole we seemed to gel and everyone appeared to support each other, if only superficially.  In  our  very  close environment cooperation was always going to be a necessity.

# Chapter Four

We arrived at Baghdad, Capital of Iraq, second largest city in the Arab world and it was extremely hot. We did not stop in Baghdad to take in any of its sights and sounds, just drove through the very flat desert in the heat. We camped in the desert that night which was not without incident.

At around 2.00 a.m. there was a 'knock' on the combi caravanette door. Menai and I got out of the combi and standing in front of us in the semi darkness were three men, dressed in ordinary clothes, one with a sten gun in his hands and the others with holstered pistols. The man with the sten gun was obviously in charge, his demeanour verging on aggressive, he spoke to us in English and was clearly aggravated. He asked us why we were camping in the desert when there were bandits about. On realising we were just visitors and travelling through, the man in charge said he would leave the two other men bedded down in the desert to watch over us and then he disappeared. The two men, our protectors who spoke no English, walked off into the night with only bed rolls and we returned to bed very unsettled.

The following morning, very bleary eyed, everyone got together for the proverbial morning coffee and we shouted just one word to our two detectives, 'Nescafe?' It was obviously a word they could relate to and understand and it was not long before they came over to join us. The other policeman from the early hours eventually turned up and took his colleagues back to wherever they had come from. We had been grateful for their presence even though their night time visit had shaken us but thankfully no incidents with bandits! Once we were organised and had packed up again we moved off, heading towards the border with Jordan.

Along the way to the border which was an extremely long road as I remember, we passed through a military zone. Iraq 1968, prior to the coming of Saddam Hussein at the time when

Hassan the dictator was in situ. We had arrived at an Army checkpoint, two vehicles that had unwittingly missed the border control point. A Captain, who we discovered spoke amazingly good English walked towards us as we were forced to stop by several concrete filled oil drums along the very dusty road. Armed guards were all around us but no other vehicles other than ourselves, like some scene out of a movie. The Captain asked for our passports and after a brief glance informed us that in fact we had actually missed the border post which was way back in the direction from which we had come, a surprise to us all as there had been no indication along our route. The Captain very kindly offered the services of one of his soldiers to accompany us to the village where the border control was in order that we could get our passports properly stamped .

Travelling back along the long sandy roads which were sprayed with crude oil to avoid the sand blowing about, we eventually arrived at the missed village where the border control office was. A gentleman came out to us dressed casually, I would think in his mid-forties. The Army guide explained to him in Arabic what had occurred and all hell let loose. At this point Menai and I and all of our fellow travellers had left our vehicles and were completely bemused by what was happening around us. The man ranted and raved at us in very good English, threatened us with imprisonment and ordered one of the guards to cock his automatic weapon which was poked into my back with some force. To say I was terrified was an understatement, the sweat pouring down my back, adrenalin pumping, heart racing and in that moment as he removed the gun from my back and stood to one side of me, for some bizarre reason all I could focus on was the fact that his weapon was stamped 'made in Czechoslovakia.' Drifting back to reality the man seemed to just rattle on and on for what seemed like an eternity and equally bizarrely just vanish with all our passports!

After a considerable and tense period, when no one dared speak or hardly dare breathe for that matter, the official re-emerged and simply said 'you are very lucky, you can go.' We were all in a state of high anxiety. No one talked, no eye to eye contact, we just sauntered back to our vehicles afraid to be seen to be rushing when in fact we wanted to run, all of us, just run for our lives. I knew that. As we left the border control post the man was still ranting, obviously someone higher in authority had overruled him and he was none too pleased. For ourselves the sense of relief was overwhelming our hearts still pounding with the thought of what had just passed. I remember a man at the passport office in Jordan asking 'glad to be out of Iraq?!' We were.

From the Jordanian border we were to travel through desert again, the road itself was tarmacked in order to service an old pipe line and the weather continued to be extremely hot. Eventually we arrived at Amman the capital, this in the days of King Hussein, who was reported to be a 'benevolent dictator.' In Amman we could find nowhere to camp and eventually resorted to camping on the outskirts in a rocky field, which was dangerous. Always the threat of bandits, it was getting dark and I recall an air of desperation amongst us all but we had no choice but to set up camp and take to our beds exhausted as ever. Sleep overcoming any anxieties.

Early in the morning we awoke to the sound of lots of noise from outside the combi and we looked out of the windows to find ourselves and the tents surrounded by people. It transpired we had set up camp in what was a Palestinian refugee camp! We had no idea whether the refugees were friendly or hostile, it was hard to gauge. Eventually however someone came along who spoke reasonable English and cleared all the people away and we explained we were visitors and just travelling through. A policeman suddenly appeared out of the blue, spoke to us in adequate English and listened to our story. He then very quickly appointed two of his officers to stay with us for the next twenty four hours. Over the next few hours one of the officers appeared more than just a little interested in our three female travellers, a little over and above his role of simply protecting us. In fact later on that night he even tried to get into their tent. We awoke to the sound of screaming and scrambled quickly out of the combi only to find the policeman making a quick exit from their tent and disappearing into the night!

The following morning a different policeman appeared, as did another well-dressed man who said he was PA to the owner of a weaving company nearby. The owner of the company had seen us and the PA said he had connections with Yorkshire and wanted to assist us, apparently the factory wove the cloth for a suit design company in Leeds of all places.What a small world!

The PA to the owner said we could camp in the grounds of the factory and could eat in their canteen if we wished with their workers. As we were having to hang around anyway whilst we waited for our VISAs for Ethiopia, we packed up and drove to the factory which was not so far away and parked up on the grass. We all felt more secure there to the point where we left the vehicles and thought we would have a walk into Amman and have a look around.

Some of us had been invited to go and have a look around one of the refugee camps which we did. The camp had been in existence since 1948. Since then during the 60's and 70's there had been several conflicts between Syria, Jordan and Israel and this was why Jordan was virtually a tourist free zone. The refugee camp was mostly canvas and we were told that the refugees had been offered materials to build brick houses but had refused, saying their homes were in Palestine (Israel) and they did not want this to be their permanent home. After our visit we made our way back to the mini bus and once again many young people had gathered around it and were visibly agitated. We said goodbye to the people who had invited us and got back in the minibus very hastily. As we started the engine, a man came towards us through the crowd of people holding a hand grenade! Down went the accelerator and we shot off out of there as quickly as we could, under a shower of rocks the children were throwing at us! We were very shocked and scared and were constantly amazed by the speed in which groups of people in this region could change so rapidly in mood. We told the PA from the factory about the visit and he was non plussed as to why we should have accepted the invitation, given the dangers. Once again, naivety, lack of knowledge and experience were giving us lessons we needed to learn and fast.

Several days later we were finally able to pick up our Visas from the Ethiopian Embassy in Amman. We said our grateful thanks to the factory owner and left once again, this time for Aqaba (of Lawrence of Arabia fame!) the only coastal city in Jordan. At this point we were joined by another traveller an Irish psychiatrist called Jim. We had arranged to meet him in Amman. Jim wanted to travel to South Africa and he said he had been a doctor working for the United Nations in some of the war torn territories of Africa.

# Chapter Five

The roads to Aqaba were long, windy mountain roads, not for those suffering from motion sickness! Very kindly, the factory owner, who was very influential in Amman had arranged for two tourist policeman to accompany us for safety. They both spoke English and suggested along the way that we should go and visit Petra.

Petra dates from around 300 BC and was the capital of the Nabatean Kingdom, tombs and temples carved into the pink sandstone cliffs, hence its nick name of 'Rose City.' In fact Petra covers 2640 acres as I understand and of course is now a World Heritage site. How could we have missed out on this? We did not. We took a diversion and went off to Petra and camped out in the grounds of a hotel inside Petra. The management gave us permission to park there, the tourist policemen slept in the local Police station in town.

Whilst we were in Petra, we did the mandatory tourist visit to the temple in the mountainside via 1000 steps. I remember it was extremely hot and the steps extremely tiring but such an interesting place. Just as an aside, we had taken a camera with us on our travels, a Russian Zenith single lens reflex to be precise and we did take a few photos on our trip to Petra, as we had in other places, but we had only a few rolls of film, so we tried to be selective where we could, though we were keen to have some record of our ramblings. We returned that day to the hotel and the two police officers took us into town as a group.

In one of the local shops, the shopkeeper who essentially sold clothing, engaged me in conversation. At some point, I cannot remember the reason why, he suddenly produced a German Luger and suggested I could hold it, very quickly one of the tourist policeman accompanying us grabbed the Luger from out of his hand and dropped the magazine which had ammunition in it, and he checked the breach before handing it over to me. I took the Luger not wanting to offend the shopkeeper who then proceeded to dress me in Bedouin clothing (for whatever reason, I assume he had plans to try and sell me something!) He told me that he had fought in the North African desert under Montgomery and had taken the luger from a German officer who was captured by them!

The following day we continued our journey to Aqaba which was then a very small town, but these days I understand a much larger resort and very popular with windsurfers!

From Aqaba we hoped to sail down the Red Sea to Ethiopia. You might question the reason why we would travel to South Africa this way, across the Middle East. Although we had only the television and newspapers for reference we were aware that there was much trouble and conflict in the Congo at that time and this was sufficient reason for us to take an alternative route.

From Aqaba our plan was to try and get a boat down the Red Sea to Massawa. Massawa had been an important port for centuries and in fact had been the capital of the Italian colony of Eretria until this was moved to Asmara in 1897. Finding a boat turned out to be much easier said than done. Had we checked this out before we would have discovered that in actual fact there were no boats stopping off at Massawa as the shipping agents informed us. In fact the agents had no idea when there would be a tramp steamer in the vicinity (a vessel that would be stopping off along the coast). There were lots of cargo ships travelling across the Indian Ocean but they were just passing through and travelling on elsewhere. So, as we had no Plan B we were forced to settle in for the long haul whilst we thought about our situation some more.

In the interim period, one of the more annoying, some would say irritating issues about our stay in Aqaba was the fact that some of the local dignitaries we came into contact with, particularly those that interacted with the women in our group, were keen to offer our female travellers marriage proposals ! Why this was we can only surmise, perhaps because they were easy prey, more available. Even I had a proposal?

We were camping at the old Saudi Arabian border post and whilst we were there we drove into Saudi with our tourist policemen and went into the new border post to see if we could be allowed to drive down to Jeddah, from where we understood we could get a cargo ferry across to Ethiopia. Unfortunately and as you might expect they said no, we had no permission from higher authorities so that was a dead end. We returned back to the campsite and spent some time looking around the area, deciding what other options we had.

In the meantime, the whole group had been invited to visit a school in the desert behind Aqaba, (the Nefud desert from where Lawrence of Arabia had attacked Aqaba with his Arab legion no less!). We all piled into the minibus and had lunch there with the tourist policemen in tow of course! The school was run by the army for Bedouin children, there was an army post nearby with Bedouin soldiers all dressed in khaki smock uniform and headgear; they were a camel brigade. The camels were all tied down, some ready for the desert, machine guns and ammunition strapped to their bodies, an extraordinary sight for us all. We had coffee in the big Army tents, cinnamon coffee which was served black and quite pleasant. We had several cups not realising that etiquette demanded that you shake your cup from side to side when you had finished. One of the tourist policeman eventually explained that they would continue to refill your cup unless you shook it! Eventually we said our goodbyes and returned to Aqaba and resumed our search for a vessel to take us down the Red Sea coast.

# Chapter Six

The following day a handful of us spent the day calling round the shipping agents again, one of whom had been to our camp and told us an interesting story about him being a 'batman' to a Lieutenant Roberts during the war, he said he still kept a photograph of him on his office desk. Lieutenant Roberts had told him that he had done such a good job as his batman that he would invite him back to Britain when he was able, but sadly that day had never come, but the agent said he lived in hope that one day it would come. To be honest we were a little sceptical about his story until the day we called back in to his office in our continued search and there on his desk was the photograph, in a frame of Lieutenant Roberts! The agent told us that he had information a Dutch owned East Indies registered coaster was coming into Aqaba soon to pick up apples and grapes from Syria. This coaster stopped at ports along the coast as far as he knew but only appeared very occasionally, its agent was in Addis Ababa. The agent said he would try and find out for us if it was calling into Massawa. We waited two long days and the agent came back to us as promised. He said the Captain of the refrigerated vessel was Dutch and that we would need to speak to the Captain first who, if agreeable to have us on board, would radio his agent in Addis to arrange a price.

Within 24 hours the Dutch coaster arrived in the port and three or four of us went on board to speak to the First Officer who was also Dutch. Trucks were arriving at the port full of apples and grapes and being loaded by crane into the holds. The First Officer took us to see the Captain who was very pleasant and both of them spoke very good English. We explained our plight to the Captain and he said it would be no problem, we could sleep out on deck on our air beds (the temperature was still very high 40 deg C or more) and the First Officer suggested they could crane lift our vehicles on top of the cargo holds and shackle them down. The Captain said he would radio the agent of the boat in Addis as he would have the last say in the matter. He asked us to return later in the day.

When we returned to the coaster, the Captain said the agent was quite affable about our travelling on board for a sum of money which was in fact very reasonable and surprised us all, then about £30.00. The boat would be stopping at Jeddah first and then Massawa. The following morning we drove down to the quayside. The First Officer organised the cranes to lift our vehicles on board, which I remember vividly being a 'heart stopping moment,' and the relief when they were on board was immense. Dangling precariously attached to what seemed like a thread at the time, the vehicles were slowly manoeuvred on board, every second I remember seemed like a lifetime. I had dark imaginings the chains would break, that the vehicles would plunge into the watery depths, never to be seen again! However all was well, we could rest easy again. The tourist policemen said goodbye to us then returned to their usual duties in Amman and our vehicles were chained down and we got on board and set sail down the Gulf of Aqaba. We were three days on the boat altogether and the sea very calm, dolphins playing about at the bow and following the boat as they do.

As we sailed down the Red Sea with Egypt on one side and the Saudi coastline on the other, we were reasonably comfortable on board, we ate our own food although there was a galley on board with a Dutch cook who was very much in charge! There were toilets and showers on the boat for the crew, the deckhands who were mostly Somali and Arab. One day I recall the American female traveller who was with us donned her bikini for a little sunbathing and was hastily reprimanded by the Captain who insisted she cover herself up, as she might offend his crew who were Muslim and not used to half naked women parading on deck, he did not need to ask her twice.

On the whole and at this time, I remember that relationships between the group remained reasonably good. Everyone seemed to be getting on well, conversation and companionship easy.

As we arrived in the port at Jeddah, a peculiar port which entailed the boat to keep dropping anchor and 'pull' itself in apparently due to the reefs. The port itself was full of pilgrim boats, the pilgrims from which were taking the 'Haj' to Mecca. The Saudi authorities made it quite plain immediately that they were most unhappy with us being on board the Dutch coaster. We were foreigners, we were not Muslim and that was sufficient for them to send local Policemen on board the ship to keep watch on us, on the seaward side to ensure we did not leave the boat. The

Captain was bemused by the whole situation and tried to placate them but the Authorities were adamant and so we sat and waited whilst the apples and grapes were unloaded. Although we could see little being on the seaward side, we did see many men dressed in loin cloths with daggers in their belts, local dress you could only assume.

The boat in front of us was full of cattle and the animals were being unloaded by crane. The stevedores on the dock were unloading the animals by tying their horns together, four cattle at a time and hoisting them on to the dock, inhumane by our standards, but that was what we were viewing, much to our consternation. The cattle dangled in mid-air as the cranes moved them out and suddenly one of the metal cables came loose and the inevitable happened, one animal dropped at least fifty to sixty feet onto the quayside, its legs clearly broken and in distress and no one doing a thing about it. For all of us it was, I remember vividly so very hard to watch, to relate to at all and when eventually all the vessel had been cleared, someone came along and cut it's throat in the Halal way and put the poor thing out of its misery, you could not help but feel entirely hopeless in the circumstances. It was a macabre memory of Jeddah and one I and probably all of us that day, will never be able to forget.

By this time our boat had been off loaded and ready to make sail. During the remainder of our trip to Massawa, I made good use of our relationship with the chief engineer of the boat in persuading him to help us fix the exhaust on the Volkswagen, which I have to say he did very happily. We travelled across the Red Sea to Massawa and the ship docked in port. Once again the crane lifted our vehicles back onto the quayside and once again our hearts were in our mouths, as they say, however all went well. We thanked the Captain and First Officer for all their assistance, shook their hands and got back into our vehicles and then passed through Customs and Immigration without incident thankfully, passports and visas intact. No one appeared interested in any

'carnets' de passage' and we drove out
of the docks and into the hills of Eritrea
to the town of Asmara.

# Chapter Seven

We arrived in Asmara, the capital town of Eritrea and everyone seemed to be coping at that point, the heat was still intense but we were getting used to it, at least 30 plus degrees every day and hats an essential. Eritrea of course is now independent of Ethiopia, Eritrea being Muslim and Ethiopia being Coptic Christian. My memory of Asmara was simply of a small town where the local Police station let us camp on the grass outside their building. We spent a couple of days there but as a group it was always the consensus of opinion mostly that determined how long we stayed in one place, always I recall a question of priorities.

It was in Asmara that we discovered the national dish of Ethiopia which was in fact 'ingera,' a fermented bread which I really could never get a taste for. We also noticed there were one or two Italian restaurants about and initially we were puzzled by this but then realised eventually that in fact Ethiopia had been invaded by Mussolini in the late 1930's, the first invasion having been during the year of 1897. Both invasions had encouraged Italian migration to the region hence there were a few Italian families that had settled there. It was also in Asmara we purchased some sulphonamide antibiotics from a local chemist, which were to prove extremely useful later on in our journey. We just had an idea there may be a day when we might need them, perhaps a psychic moment?

Although Ethiopia has a 13th month calendar, we actually left Asmara on the 5th November by our calendar and I remember we heard fireworks that day in the distance, from somewhere, we had no idea where exactly or for what reason in that place, not to celebrate Guy Fawkes surely ?

It was a two day journey to Addis along tarmac but windy roads which had been built by the Italians up into the mountains. As far as we knew there were no 'bandits' on this particular stretch of our journey. Once again the question would be where to stop. We knew we had to cross the Blue Nile Gorge, another spectacular sight, part of the Rift Valley where two tectonic plates meet. Deep and cavernous with a substantial river thundering down its middle, there was a substantial bridge we needed to cross patrolled by armed guards and I remember some of our fellow travellers dropping stones over the edge of the gorge just for a bit of fun essentially as we were so high up. On arrival at the bridge, which was half way down the gorge, it was getting very dark and we had to camp soon however the land around the bridge was full of scorpions, the small dangerous variety! We had no choice though, so with extreme care and vigilance we put up our tents, constantly checking for the dreaded scorpions.

As you can imagine no one got much sleep that night. The tents had zip doors and sewn in ground sheets so we thought everyone would be reasonably safe. Menai and I slept in the combi only bedding down after an unexpected display of two praying mantis mating on the wing mirror! The female, as they are want devouring the male at the end when all was done and dusted! A thought and a vision to sleep on, if sleep had been possible.

Having explored the top of the gorge a little earlier, we discovered it was extremely cold at night but inside the gorge itself where we were camped, the heat of the day was held in the rocks so in fact it remained warm until the following morning. The night was uneventful and we packed up very carefully in the morning, ensuring no scorpion had infiltrated our kit ! Once we were ready to go we crossed the steel girder bridge, noting en route that the Blue Nile was in fact dirty brown!

As we ascended uphill and higher into the mountains the Ford Transit began to splutter and we feared the worst. It was later said to us that the reason for this was that the oxygen was too thin to produce proper fuel/air mix, but as we descended into the lowlands, the Ford settled down again thankfully and all was well.

We reached Addis Ababa eventually and again we discussed where to camp. Once again we made our way to the local Police HQ, as this had been successful previously and fortunately this time too. The Police Chief himself came over to chat to us and give us advice, he spoke very good English and even invited all of us to his house for a meal, which we were extremely glad to accept.

We pitched our tents on the grassed lawn at the back of the Police HQ and stayed there about three days. It was in Addis that the famous box of biscuits we had bought at the start of our journey  suddenly became the subject of much discontent in our group just a small thing, a box of biscuits that had taken up a lot of space sadly became the focus of everyone's general frustration and agitation. One evening, one of our fellow travellers the ex-postmistress asked us if they could have some of our cookies, we said yes of course and handed the box of biscuits over to them. The biscuits had never been 'ours,' they had been bought for all to share something for everyone. Menai and I were uncomfortably aware of feeling segregated from the group, albeit not intentionally but I remember it was a difficult time. We felt unable to resolve the situation, everyone's frustrations clearly tangible and we had a personal sense of being disowned, the biscuits being the 'touch paper.'

In those few days Menai and I met up with an American couple who had a Volkswagen Combi camper like ours. I remember their names were Nancy and Lou, they told us they were zoologists. He was doing a research project in East Africa and they had come to the Police HQ as someone had told them there were some English people camped at the station! Nancy and Lou were staying in Ethiopia at the time but were travelling through to Kenya, as we were.

After three days we decided it was time to move on and we travelled on to the town of Aksum, which at the time housed the crown jewels of Haile Selassie, Emperor of Ethiopia. The jewels were held in the Coptic cathedral. In Aksum once again we struggled to find somewhere to camp and eventually arrived at a local hotel. We asked if we could camp on their land and they said yes as long as we paid four Ethiopian dollars every time we used the toilet! We decided this was a step too far and ended up camping in the grounds of the local prison instead. The Commander of the prison, who spoke good English was happy to have us camp there and even had the prisoners come out to clear and clean the grass up first before we pitched up!

The Commander had given us permission to use the staff toilets in the prison and there was also a well for fresh water in the grounds. We were all mesmerised by the sight of a young girl no more than 6-7 years of age who had half a car tyre inner tube at the end of the rope which she plunged into the well and then emptied the water into her bucket. She threw it in with ease, hauled it up again with speed and dexterity which amazed us all. Her technique impressive.

Around Aksum dotted around the landscape were monoliths, some fallen down, but inscribed with script from 2-3,000 years BC. The modern cathedral was in the middle of town. We thought it might be a problem getting to see the crown jewels, however there was a monk there who spoke no English, but we said the words 'crown jewels' to him and he nodded and gestured us in and to sit down on some pews at the front of the cathedral. I remember there were very few chairs. We all sat down and the monk reappeared with some others, a trolley and a thick cloth. The door of the trolley was unlocked, the cloth laid on the floor before us and the 'crown jewels' placed on the cloth by the monks, no security in those days ! We smiled and admired the jewels and even picked them up. It was quite unbelievable, I remember the jewels were something to behold. All the monks required was a donation to the cathedral. At the end of the display the jewels were loaded back up in to the trolley and taken away to wherever they were stored. The monks bowed and left. It was an interesting visit and we felt quite honoured.

In Aksum there were a lot of walks and footpaths in the area however we did not have any time to explore. At this point along our journey, the group were becoming exhausted, mainly due to the length of time it had taken to get only this far. Everyone seemed 'tetchy' and 'edgy' understandably and most of their frustration directed at me as organiser of the trip. Fortunately Menai and myself were able to cope with the pressure and were empathetic, knowing my own lack of experience was the main reason and time was pressing.

From a practical point of view, clothes were changed infrequently on our journey, occasionally washed by hand and in those days of course no ready supply of bottled water, just jerry cans that we topped up along the way. We used iodine tablets to purify the water and in many ways just made it up as we were going along. Toilet facilities other than on the official campsites were literally just a hole in the ground and as I recall the men spent most of the time with five o'clock shadows, given we only had battery operated shavers. It was just easier not to bother most of the time.

## Chapter Eight

Ethiopia was hilly and mountainous and an experience for all. The existence of 'roads' as such were simply modified tracks made by a constant traffic of people and animals. The reality was that it literally poured down the whole time we were travelling thorough the region, hence the muddy roads, torrential rain, rain as I recall like stair rods, thunder, lightning, the whole gambit and of course it was November the rainy season.

Once we had seen the main sights of Aksum we got moving again. There was much to see in Ethiopia but we needed to get to the Kenyan border that was the priority. Kenya unlike Ethiopia was relatively flat despite having a mountain range, Mount Kenya being the highest. However in between times we decided to visit Lake

Tarna. It was said at the time that the islands in Lake

Tarna had the biggest pythons in Africa, whether this was true or not thankfully we never got to find out! We arrived at Lake Tarna looking down on the spectacular falls with their 300 ft drop where you could feel the spray on your face in the heat of the day from the top of the hill. All around were Ethiopian tribesmen dressed in loin cloths, carrying Italian carbines, rifles from the 1930's, which were seen as a prestige item? We had been told that there was a hydroelectric dam at Lake Tarna and we stayed there one night. The scheme was managed by an Englishman.

Tunnelled into the stone of the Blue Nile, were 'halls' where turbines and generators had been placed, halls where we were able to walk into. There were also toilets and showers which we were able to use, what joy. The Manager told us that the carbines the tribesmen were carrying were extremely dangerous and that the barrels would just split if ever they were fired, it was certainly a memorable visit.

Just as an aside in this travelog, I would mention that we noticed that in some of the shops in Ethiopia and Kenya there were bags of rice and corn and also farming tools with a stamp on the side saying ' gift from the people of the USA' obviously charitable goods which should have been given out for free, but in fact were being sold? We can only assume that then as now corruption is ever present.

Another overnight stop was also required this time at the Sudan Interior

Mission station. We gained entry through the main gate which had a bell at the front. We rang the bell and waited. After a while we heard the faint 'put-put' sound of a small motorcycle and around the corner behind the gate appeared a burly bearded man (who happened to be an American) riding a BSA Bantam motorcycle 125 cc. He opened the gates and as I recall was not very welcoming by any standards but we politely asked whether we could camp in their grounds. There was a large grassed area outside and he said we could park over on the other side of it as long as we did not speak to anyone, or move outside our camp under any circumstances? A little strange we thought but we did as he asked and set up camp. We saw a few people walking around with bibles, learning later it was a Bible Study Centre. Since then I have been told that some of those Missions were a front for the CIA and some in Brazil were actually closed down, whether this one was we would never get to discover.

Dusk was approaching and suddenly out of the dusk a man and a woman appeared, they were Canadian Baptist missionaries. Unlike the bearded man, the couple were very pleasant and invited us all back to their flat in the grounds. We explained we had been told not to move from camp, but they said not to worry. The wife had baked two cakes and we all had an interesting evening talking about Ethiopia and mission life. We sampled some of the food her husband had brought in locally, much of which was fermented cereal which was not to everyone's palate sadly, but we spent a good three hours in their company and then returned back to our campsite and to bed. The following morning the familiar sound of the motorcycle was heard and the bearded man appeared once again like a vision checking we were packed up and ready to leave. He waited and then after we left closed the gate behind us as quickly as he could. Clearly he was glad to see the back of us.

The road that we had travelled on to the campsite was essentially just cinders, not metalled, it had been adequate to travel on. However from this point onwards the road thankfully changed to a wide tarmaced road, which meant we could get some speed up finally. Along this stretch of road we knew we had to turn off at some point for the Kenyan border, but the maps we had with us were very unclear so we kept driving until it was nearly dark. Eventually we came to a road maintenance depot and we drove inside the walls and asked if we could camp there overnight. Across the road from the depot was a garage belonging to the road maintenance depot. The man in charge of the garage spoke good English and I asked him for directions to the border. He simply pointed out of the window and said 'over there' which was directly across from the depot. The road was a combination of farm track and rocky footpath the sort you might find in the Derbyshire Dales, my heart sank as the reality was that our vehicles were clearly not built for that sort of terrain. In that moment I thought we were finished, I thought it was all over and that we could not possibly contemplate navigating that track. I had dark imaginings of wheels coming off and axles breaking if we took the farm track road out, a complete dilemma. I returned to the group and we discussed our options. Some of our fellow travellers were extremely agitated, understandably so but thankfully no one came to blows, frustration and despair just hanging in the air. After quite some time the decision was made that we should just 'go for it,' but very, very slowly.

It was at this point on our journey that Jim the psychiatrist who had joined us in Amman suddenly produced some cartons of Valium and Mogadon (sleeping tablets) he had brought with him. Given the stress we were all under he thought they might be helpful and in fact when things became more difficult and relationships strained, some of our group, including myself, did take a few if only to retain some calm and remain sane! Sleep did not come easily.

## Chapter Nine

The following morning we set off along the farm track road, the trouble being that there were lots of other tracks going off right and left and we had no idea where they led. We just kept going in a straight line as far as we could. We travelled for hours and eventually night came and we were forced to camp in the bush and hope for the best. Thankfully the night was uneventful and we carried on the following day stopping only for a drink and something to eat.

As luck or fate would have it, as we had stopped for a bit of a break on this unruly path, an army truck suddenly appeared and stopped to check us out. One of the soldiers got out of the truck to speak to us, fortunately he spoke a little English and we explained we were on our way to Kenya. There were soldiers in the back of the truck and they were en route back to the army camp outside a nearby village. The soldier told us to follow their tracks which would take us to the village, so we got back into the vehicles and set off behind them. Coming to the village as I recall was a complete relief. The military camp was camouflaged on the other side of the village and the Commander came over to see us pointing out that we were not equipped for this sort of journey and terrain, which was blindingly obvious to all. We knew that! He explained there were two ways to the Kenyan border, one way was not a proper graded road and was a mud bath if it rained. The other track had been naturally made by tribesmen who had walked it over many years, probably centuries. The soldiers were apparently going to the border themselves to an airstrip used by Ethiopia and Kenya and the Commander suggested we could follow their tracks again and we thanked him for his assistance. They were leaving for Moyale in two days' time.

In the village we found a man who made bread in a stone 'pizza' type oven and I think he must have thought all his Christmases had come at once as we bought all his bread that day! There was a water pump in the village which had a petrol driven pump to bring the water up. Once a day all the villagers filled their cans and containers as we did, however the water was very 'brackish' and not pleasant but it was all we had and we had to make the most of it.

Again call it fate, good fortune whatever, that night the heavens opened in grand style almost a monsoon. The rain was copious and heavy and had collected in the folds of the tarpaulin tied between the two vehicles. In the morning when all was quiet once again, we channelled all the water from the top of the tarpaulin into a bucket and drank that instead, nectar from above it seemed at the time I remember.

The following day we rested. In the late morning an open topped 'Land Rover' suddenly appeared in the village with four young Scottish men, who were very chatty and amiable. They said they had come from a different direction than ourselves but they had got lost too. Unlike ourselves they were clearly on a mission and took off again without stopping, to who knows where, their enthusiasm was tangible and we suspected they were just making it up as they went along?

The next morning we awoke to hear the sounds of the Army truck getting ready to leave the village and so we quickly packed up and began to follow the tracks as suggested. Little did we know but the old road was not properly graded and very soon we became bogged down and stuck in the mud, unable to move. Wheels were spinning quite unable to gain any purchase, the rain incessant and all of us soaked to the skin, we were getting nowhere fast. Once again we were desperate for some help from somewhere.  Fortunately for us a jeep and a 'Land Rover' appeared carrying what turned out to be an English doctor, who told us he was doing research for the UN, something to do with malaria control and also an American entomologist with two assistants. Very kindly they came and helped to pull us out of the mud but in doing so their 'Land Rover' got stuck. There were frustrations all round as you might envisage but finally with lots of input , they hooked their jeep up to the 'Land Rover' and got that out too with some effort. We could not believe how lucky we were again that we were all travelling that road at such an apt moment.

Once again we set off very slowly through the mire.  The road was extremely rough and the Transit kept getting caught up on the uneven rocky surface. We had to keep stopping to dig the Transit wheels out with spades in order to keep the vehicle moving. In actual fact the Volkswagen combi did much better than the Transit on those bad roads which I never would have imagined. We were all very tired and all very weary by the end of that day and because of having made such slow progress we ended up camping very roughly in the bush. Sleep came very easily that night. The next day we eventually reached another village which had a Norwegian Lutheran Mission. The missionary by his manner indicated that he was not at all happy about us being there but he did allow us to camp on their site as long as 'we did not damage the flowers?' We stayed just the one night and then drove off very early the next morning. After a short time we came upon a very narrow wooden bridge that was quite obviously rotting and I remember it was more than just a little hair raising getting the vehicles over it to say the least. An inch at a time both vehicles 'crept' along the wooden slats, all of us holding our breath till we reached the other side. After that the track did improve, the surface was firmer, but we were still only doing 10-15 miles an hour and still making snail's progress.

Finally we reached the border between Ethiopia and Kenya at Moyale. There was a shallow river between the two but no bridge, the water was low and therefore passable. Passport Control appeared disinterested, no mention of 'carnet de passages' and so we set off across the river bed, very slowly as I recall and up the other side to Kenya. It was quite a narrow ford not much of an obstacle though if it had been full of flood water it may have been. Thankfully we were soon across and then followed a short steep climb, both vehicles having survived without incident.

# Chapter Ten

The town of Moyale was divided between Kenya and Ethiopia both very different areas. The Kenyan side essentially a Muslim town was quiet and reserved and the Ethiopian side Coptic Christian hence it had a far more relaxed demeanour, for example there were bars and numerous other 'services' including prostitutes as we were told.

In Moyale there was a Mosque made of stone and slate and the rest of the buildings were simply mud huts. The Army/Police compound had a barbed wire fence that surrounded the compound with very large gates and guards on both sides, but we drove through and were not challenged. Kenya had been a British colony and on the whole everything seemed much better organised this side of the border and just as an aside we noticed that the soldiers and the police all had creases down the front of their trousers, all very tailored. We were guided to the

Chief Superintendent's office. The Chief Superintendent was a big man I remember, about 6ft 5" very pleasant with a helpful disposition and he looked at our passports and said we could camp opposite the prison where there were toilets on site, extremely basic as they were! That night we camped outside the prison and for the first time in a long time we felt as if we were back amongst a group of people we could relate to. It somehow felt very 'British' even to the point of the soldiers parading every morning, as early as 7.30 a.m. dressed in pressed uniform. There was a sense of an historical British presence, compared to some of the localities we had come through.

One night after we arrived in Moyale (Kenya), we walked back into Moyale (Ethiopia) which we had decided to explore earlier on in the evening. It was quite a 'lively' place at night prostitutes walking around freely. We were strolling along an extremely dark dirt road back to our camp and along the way we suddenly heard a loud 'roar' and we were literally terrified, I remember we ran 'hell for leather ' back down the road through the gates to camp. The next day, the Chief of Police got us altogether, he had heard about our visit to Moyale (Ethiopia) and quite frankly gave us a 'telling off.' He said we should never have gone over the border into Ethiopia and that if we had got into trouble, he would not have been able to help us, we had been well and truly warned.

Another day whilst at the Police/Army facility, I remember a German man appeared with a black man, they had been driving across Africa having come from South Africa in a Mercedes saloon. The black man had hitched a lift along the way and they had apparently got stuck in a mud pool as you might expect in a Mercedes saloon! The German man had left his friend with the vehicle and he and the black traveller had walked overnight (unbelievable, given bush and snakes on both sides of the track) to the border to get help. The Army eventually took one of their trucks out and went to rescue the vehicle, it was somehow comforting to know that other people were having similar issues to ourselves, once again due to travelling in unsuitable vehicles.


In Moyale, a young boy attached himself to our group, he spoke a little English and said he needed money, he appeared extremely emaciated. Whilst we were in camp the boy used to translate for us and in return we would give him some food and other bits and pieces. I remember giving him one of my T-shirts which was obviously much too big for his little frame but he took it from me with enthusiasm. Menai and myself were surprised that the young boy never ever said thank you for anything or in fact ever said please either for that matter. It was only later in Marsabit that one of the Missionaries who spoke his language explained that 'please' and 'thank you' did not exist in their language, there was no need for it. The Rendille people of Kenya, whose name out of interest translates as 'Holders of the Stick of God', were a community who expected to share everything without acknowledgement. The missionary did ask us whether he gave us a gift when we left Moyale and we said yes he had given us a small pot, made from the bark of a tree and cured with urine ! He explained that was their way of showing appreciation for assistance. He said that if the Rendille people had felt someone had gone over and above their duty this was normal practice. It was this same boy who told us that locals who lived in Moyale believed the local charitable pharmacy 'watered down' their medications and because of this belief they preferred to borrow money from money lenders to go over the border into Ethiopia and actually purchase drugs they believed were 'the real thing.' We talked to the Army doctor about this and he said that the drugs in the charitable pharmacy were exactly the same as the ones they were purchasing over the border. His explanation and belief was that some of the liquid pharmaceuticals were in concentrated form and had to be diluted in order to be usable. He thought this had been witnessed by someone in the past and somehow become an urban legend.

After two days of rest we noticed other travellers appearing at Moyale from all directions mostly in 'Land Rover's we noted, the correct vehicles for this terrain undoubtedly! Some travellers stayed overnight, others just travelled through. Amongst the travellers we met up with who stayed a while were Michael and Seamus who were Irish chicken farmers. Seamus sat and read us poetry at nights, Michael busy elsewhere with the 'loose' women over the border in Ethiopia! Michael used to return drunk and sang Irish folk songs. I remember him standing at the main entrance shouting loudly 'Michael here!' and the guard actually running off! Seamus was clearly embarrassed by the whole scenario.

It was whilst we were camped in Moyale Menai had a problem with her foot. A jigger flea had laid eggs in the corner of her big toe! We had been told about the parasite bugs we might encounter on route and Menai unfortunately had been wearing open toed sandals and it was obvious to us both there was a problem. We spoke to the Asian Army doctor again who diagnosed the problem and said he would have to clean out the infection. A Somali nurse sprayed her toe with some sort of cocaine based spray and continued spraying it until the doctor, who left some seriously ill patients to attend to Menai  arrived to clean out the wound, a little unfair we thought given a minor issue but Menai was very grateful nonetheless. Note to readers, open toed sandals not recommended in this region!

It became blatantly obvious at Moyale that some members of our group were very clearly irritated by the length of time it had taken to reach this point and had noticeably become disinterested, unmotivated and despairing at how problematic the journey had become. Some members of the group had noticed that private aeroplanes had landed on the air strip at Moyale, on enquiry they were scheduled air taxis from Wilson Airport Nairobi.  One of the females in our group wanted to go to Nairobi, she had always planned to go there anyway and she and the psychiatrist who wanted to return to Ireland decided that they would take the air taxi. This then set a precedent for the others in our group and one by one they decided to leave us and move on elsewhere. They were exhausted, we were exhausted mentally and physically, but as we had the two vehicles to look after there was no escape for ourselves, we had to carry on.

It seemed strange when eventually there were just the two of us, but we understood completely that the other travellers had had enough. The last to leave was an Australian called Nick who in actual fact had got himself a job with a drilling company operating on the outskirts of Moyale. In some ways it was a relief that we were finally on our own but we had grown stronger by all that we had endured so far. We had said our goodbyes to each one but sadly without affinity for our fellow travellers. No promises to keep in touch that was just how it ended not what we had envisaged and in retrospect regrettable and disappointing. It was a sad time for both of us.

It was just after the last of our fellow travellers left that Menai and I were invited to a film show at the Army camp nearby, a bit of a distraction as we were feeling a bit low at the time understandably. As we sat down in the brick built hall waiting for the film to begin, lots of cans of beer were being passed around before and during the show which to be honest we very much enjoyed. The following day, one of the Somali men who had been giving out the cans of beer came to our camp and presented us with a chit for 'our round,' the previous night! We were taken back but not wanting to lose face we settled the bill straight away, despite the fact that no one had mentioned a thing about chits for these drinks at the time!

A few days later and quite out of the blue Nancy and Lou from Addis Ababa appeared in their Volkswagen combi! It was good to see them and sort of took the edge off our current situation. Nancy and Lou were on their way to see Jo Adamson (of Born Free fame) who was running a leopard breeding programme, sadly he was later murdered by Somali bandits. We had a couple of days with them which was a welcome distraction and gave us something else to think about, but as ever our reunion was too short lived and Nancy and Lou disappeared off on their travels once again. We were sad to see them go we had got on with each other so very well.

After they left and whilst still in Moyale, I had eaten some of the local food and very quickly become extremely ill to the point of being delirious. Menai was very concerned that I had deteriorated so rapidly and ran across to the Army doctor at the camp nearby. He came to see me straight away and found me lying down in the combi virtually comatose. The doctor believed I had malaria however quinine and other medications he gave me made no difference at all. Having no other choice the doctor and some of the soldiers carried me unceremoniously to the local 'hospital.' The makeshift hospital was clean but there were no window frames, it was very basic, old style metal framed hospital beds, sheets and lots of bug powder!

Menai told me later that the local tribesman had got up from their beds on the ward though sick themselves, spears propped up against their bed heads, they had made the effort to stand around my bed holding my hand and laid their hands on my forehead, shaking their heads, something I was vaguely aware of in my delirium . In my confused state I remember hearing them whispering to each other obviously in a language I did not understand but I was aware they were there. Menai told me that they had also held her hand and spoke to her gently, though she did not understand the words she understood their sentiments and was very moved by this and would remember these moments for a long time to come.

The Army doctor apparently told Menai that I was going to die and for whatever reason as destiny would have it perhaps Menai suddenly remembered the sulphonamide antibiotics we had purchased earlier on our journey and she started to feed me with them. Within twenty four hours I became stable again, I was still feverish but I had not got worse and so she continued to give them to me and very quickly I started to come round. I still had terrible diarrhoea but I was not delirious. I had lost a lot of weight in those three days and the doctor advised not to eat any of the local food. Menai had saved my life and by the fourth day I really started to pick up again. It had been a surreal experience and I would be eternally grateful to Menai and everyone else for keeping me alive. The relief was immense and before I left I managed to say a weak thank you in English to all the other sick people in their beds who had supported me. Even though they did not understand what I was saying I believed they sensed it.

The Chief Superintendent of Police had apparently heard about how ill I had been and he said we could sleep in his bungalow, which was extremely thoughtful of him. I remember the beds were covered with white anti bug powder which was a little off putting but I really needed to rest, I had so little energy. Very slowly I began to recover and get my strength back. Menai and I spent several days at the bungalow, playing scrabble at night with the Police chief and his Inspector who was a terrible cheat! Before we left the Chief Superintendent showed much interest in our Grundig radio which was battery operated and as we were leaving we said he could have it. He was extremely grateful and insisted on paying us £10.00 for it, a small price to pay for all those entertaining nights of scrabble perhaps?

Whilst we were still in Moyale and just as an aside, prior to our setting out for South Africa I recall I had a heavy duty army jacket that I had bought in an Army Surplus Store. To my amazement it was a real 'hit' with the police and soldiers who all had similar jackets, but not of the same quality and to my amusement, I was continually being offered all sorts of money and other items for it. Eventually I had to stop wearing it but still they came, having seen me in it, with their bids of this and that. I had no choice I had to hide it and tell them I had given it away to someone!

# Chapter Eleven

As soon as I was fully recovered Menai and I finally left Moyale. We had heard the road ahead was not good, rutted in fact, which we anticipated would be a huge problem for the Transit. Menai was going to drive the combi and I would drive the Transit and so we packed up and said our goodbyes and had only travelled about four miles down the road, an uneven road with very high banks. On the downhill stretch of road suddenly the combi veered up the side of the embankment and turned over. I leapt out of the Transit and pulled Menai out, thankfully she was not hurt just a bit shocked and bruised understandably. We got back into the Transit and went back to the camp and we told them we needed help to get the combi back on its wheels. Again and quite fortunately an Army truck full of soldiers was about to travel down that road and they said they would get the combi up, which they did. The combi was in a poor state very battered but it was still driveable by some miracle. The soldiers left and we returned back to the camp once again. When we returned we met an Israeli couple who had been hitching lifts to Moyale. I explained to them what had happened to us and the fact that Menai was now not confident driving the combi. The husband said he would be prepared to drive it and even though we knew very little about the couple, it seemed a good plan. Two African men in the camp had a 'Land Rover,' they were getting specimens for a company and said they would come with us and so we set off driving very slowly over the ruts. All of a sudden the clutch went on the Transit. The 'Land Rover' stopped and they said they would tow us. However this was at 'Land Rover' speed! The front axle hit a couple of tree stumps as we sped along the road, the combi behind us somewhere in the distance. They had disappeared.

Eventually we arrived in a small village and when I got under the Transit I realised a spring had come off the pedal, once I had fixed that all was well again. In the village there was a police station and a Roman Catholic mission.

We went into the police station and explained what had happened and that we had lost our combi with the Israeli couple. The Police said they were sorry but they had no fuel for their truck and asked one of the two African men who had towed us whether they could borrow their 'Land Rover', which they were very reluctant to do as they had very little fuel either. I had a little in the Transit in a jerry can which we then poured into the Land Rover tank.

Once we were ready the policemen emerged from the police station donned in battledress with rifles and a Bren gun! Why the guns we asked? 'shifter men' the policeman said, Somali bandits. He explained that they had to keep watch for them as they would appear at intervals mostly pinching cattle.

We all piled into the 'Land Rover' and went back down the road and there was the combi, some way back, stuck on a mound of earth, the wheels off the ground and it was getting dark. The Israeli couple were sat inside, having lit a candle to celebrate a Jewish festival!! We were lost for words……

The police pushed the combi off the mound and we all eventually drove back to the village. We went to the Roman Catholic mission which was Italian and we were welcomed, in fact they even offered us their guest house. We stayed overnight and then continued on our way to Marsabit with the Israeli couple driving the combi and Menai and myself in the Transit. The road had improved a little which meant we could move along a bit faster. However on route to Marsabit one of the tyres shredded on the combi but we did have a spare wheel and so we put that on and continued our journey. Then we had no spare wheel. Sadly we had little interaction with the Israeli couple, all just focussed on getting from A to B, as quickly as we could. The roads from Moyale to Marsabit were rutted and muddy just a track through the bush essentially. The occasional Dik-Dik (small deer) or snake slithering across our path. It was challenging as ever.

A few miles before we got into Marsabit, we bumped into an Army convoy. The commander of the convoy said that we should stay with them because of Somali bandits in the area, so as requested we travelled along with them into the small town of Marsabit, along a few more bone jarring roads.

Marsabit now almost surrounded by the Marsabit National Park still semi desert, with lots of old volcanic activity, craters etc. one of the more remote outposts of Kenya was a tribal melting pot as we understood. As was par for the course, we headed for the police post as always, looking for somewhere to camp. They said we could camp out in their grounds, but in the meantime someone told us that the Church of England Mission was just outside of town, this was a medical mission. The policeman at the post said 'I see shifter men did not get you!!' Thankfully we had seen no bandits at all. We then drove over to the Mission with the Israeli couple to check it out. Having stopped outside we went up to the prefab house which was the

Mission, the Church was just a shack with a corrugated iron roof. We knocked at the door and a lady came out to speak to us, she was extremely pleasant and said we could park in the field outside, which we did. Once we were settled the Israeli couple said that they wanted to leave in the morning to travel down South and I said no, that we needed to stay a while and rest, this clearly aggravated both of them and they left the camp to look for a truck in the town that might be travelling South so they could hitch a lift. As they never returned that day, we assumed that they must have found a lift somewhere, they literally disappeared, obviously on their own mission.

The lady who had welcomed us on arrival at the Mission had explained that it was her husband's hospital. When we met him he was sadly quite hostile and said he was a mission doctor not a missionary. The missionary himself was an ex-Army chaplain who lived in the bungalow next door and thankfully he was slightly more welcoming than the doctor had been.

We had been told that the mission doctor's two children, both boys were at boarding school in Nairobi and they later flew into Marsabit on an air taxi for the Christmas holidays to be with their parents.

Marsabit was a small brick town with one little shop I remember that sold only spaghetti, tomato puree and tinned peas! You could get petrol and diesel from a hand pump in town. We had a walk around later in the day and the following morning the missionary doctor's wife came to invite us for lunch. They apparently ate food from their allotment but even so we thought we ought to contribute something so Menai and myself went to the local shop and bought some tinned peas as they were the only food item available! At lunch time we went over to the house and she had set the table for us. We sat down and waited for her husband who was returning for lunch and when he saw us sitting there his face spoke a thousand words. He was not a happy man and the next hour or so proved extremely uncomfortable, his wife explaining she had invited us over for lunch. All her husband had to say was 'have they contributed' and of course we had, 'tinned peas' she said. The silence was deafening and in fact I recall the only dialogue we had with her husband was him complaining about having no money. There was little other conversation otherwise and we were relieved when lunch was over and we could leave having thanked his wife who had done her best in a challenging situation. It must not have been easy.

In Marsabit there were lots of footpaths around the area but once again as time was pressing we had no time to explore them we just needed to move on. I remember there was also a fenced reserve close by housing a herd of rhinos, something else we never had the chance to check out. In the town itself there was a blacksmith who made armlets and beads for the local natives. He had a young boy working with him and I remember Menai and myself stood and watched as the young boy pumped air into two leathery looking cow's stomachs to keep the temperature up in the forge! Not a pretty sight. The young boy looked no more than six to eight years old and it must have been exhausting.

During our short stay in Marsabit, we learned that Nancy and Lou were parked up at the Police post in their Volkswagen combi! We were pleased to see them again and explained about our predicament and the fact we now had no spare wheel/tyre. Someone told us that an air taxi came to Marsabit twice weekly and suggested that if we spoke to the pilot and gave him some money then he might be able to get us a spare wheel/tyre and bring it back with him on his next flight. So the following day we spoke to the pilot, he said okay and we gave him some money. The following week the air taxi arrived with a different pilot who said he knew nothing about it, he said we should have gone to the agent for Boscovitch Airlines in the town and arranged it with him.

As you might imagine we were then stuck in Marsabit for yet another week and were no further forward. However, in the meantime we had met an American man who was teaching at a secondary school up in the hills away from town, a boarding school.  He said he was planning to leave in the next ten days, hoping to get an air taxi back to Nairobi, but after we had explained our situation, he offered to drive the combi back for us! Menai was much relieved the pressure was off.

# Chapter Twelve

Christmas was approaching and Nancy and Lou were still camping at Marsabit. Lou offered us one of his wheels as he had two spares which we accepted gratefully. During our conversation at the time we told them that we had met an American who was a teacher, I recall of sciences. We explained that he had offered to drive the combi back for us.

In between times the American had asked if he could give the chief of another village a lift back and we said yes of course. The mission doctor's wife was busy at that time making a Christmas cake and was also in the process of making another smaller cake, which she said she was giving to friends. Menai helped her make the cake filling in a little time before we were to leave. Prior to us leaving the doctor had become a little friendlier in that period and talked to me about his hobby which was mountain climbing and asked if I would like to accompany him on a climb. I said yes of course not realising what I was letting myself in for, I was just glad that we had formed something of a relationship, or at least he was tolerating us. He took Menai and myself out in the 'Land Rover' to show us some volcanic craters. Not unexpectedly perhaps we got lost along the way, as seemed commonplace in this area and the missionary who was with us asked us if we could use a compass!! Menai stayed in the 'Land Rover' whilst I circumnavigated the craters with the doctor. Suffice to say I ripped my shirt on devil's thorns scrambling back out of the crater and was glad to get out in one piece. Eventually we found our way back home, after much deliberation between the doctor and missionary, I was merely a bystander. After quite some time we arrived back at the mission station with a sense of relief.

Towards Christmas there was an Islamic festival in town. A bull had been brought in to be slaughtered and the doctor asked us to move our vehicles in the field to make room for the festival, as the animal would need to be bled and blessed before it was fit for eating. Menai and myself did as asked and witnessed this most barbaric scene. It was very hard to watch and most upsetting but quite normal for everyone else. We noticed the doctor was not at all fazed by this carnage and explained to his sons quite pragmatically what they were viewing.

Christmas Day dawned and there was a knock at the door and the two sons of the doctor were standing there and they had a parcel in their hands, wrapped in Christmas paper from the doctor's wife. It was the small Christmas cake she had said was for friends. We thanked the children and were quite overwhelmed by her thoughtfulness. So we cut the cake in half and walked over to the Police compound and offered the other half of the cake to Nancy and Lou as a gift for Christmas. In return they had, unbeknown to us bought me a neckerchief and beads from the local blacksmith for Menai.

The mission doctor's children appeared out of their parent's bungalow on Christmas morning. One of them was dressed in his Christmas present, a cowboy outfit with a pistol which he was very proud to show off to us (which somehow seemed incongruous to us his father being a Christian doctor) and the other boy had been given a model sailing boat. Later that day we drove out to a small pond where the native cattle drank, the doctor informed us that it was probably full of parasitic worms however the young boy just waded out with bare feet to sail his boat! Menai and I were most concerned about the worms but his father just shrugged and said 'they are easily got rid of' and let him carry on much to our concern.

It was then Christmas night and the mission doctor's wife said she was having a party and asked us whether we would like to come. Of course there was no alcohol, just orange juice and tomato juice, which her husband decanted into wine glasses as if a spirit. Several senior policeman came to the party, dressed in suits. We sat and watched the story of Jesus of Nazareth on slides (obviously intended for children) and there were games after (obviously intended for children too). The party ended when the doctor said we needed to pack up and call it a day. Within thirty seconds it seemed, everyone had disappeared?  It was quite an experience!

The following day the American appeared and we organised to leave the next day. We said our goodbyes to Nancy and Lou who were still doing research and our other travelling companion 'the Chief' appeared the next day, complete with spear and covered in ochre paint dressed in the usual loin cloth. He sat in the front of the combi with the American, the spear between his legs. Having said our thanks to our hosts at the mission we set off and on route, dropped off 'the Chief' at his village.

Not long after we had dropped the chief off we had a puncture in the combi but thankfully we had the spare wheel. The next thing we had to navigate was a river with a concrete ford which had been blown up by bandits. It was very rocky and the Transit inevitably got stuck in the mud, wheels spinning, we thought we were doomed. As fate would have it a 'Land Rover' appeared, driven by a lecturer in geology from Leeds University! He managed to pull us out only to get stuck himself, as seemed to be the way of things in this neck of the woods. Fortunately he had a Tanganyika jack which fitted under the rear bumper and with some extreme manual effort lifted the 'Land Rover' up. We put stones underneath, which gave him just enough purchase to drive the vehicle out and up onto the bank. The American reversed the combi, put his foot down on the throttle and did not get stuck at all. Yet another great escape was had by all!

After all the excitement of the day we decided to stop for the night. The lecturer from Leeds carried on with his journey and then quite out of the blue the five Scottish lads from Ethiopia appeared again. They were still in good spirits still on a quest and camped overnight with us, the lads plus thousands of mosquitoes that swamped us. Thankfully we had all taken our anti-malarial tablets but we had no nets, we just sprayed everywhere! The Scottish lads left early and seemed oblivious to anything really, they were just having a good time, unperturbed and in good humour.

We packed up some time later and continued our journey along a fairly decent dirt road until we had to cross a small muddy bottomed river. The Transit got stuck again. Fortunately, four local tribesman, who spoke no English dressed simply in loin cloths, large earrings and holding spears just appeared from out of nowhere. They came over and helped us push the vehicle out onto a harder surface and we were then able to drive out of the river back onto the dirt road. In the process, the tribesmen got covered in mud from the spinning wheels, they indicated purely be gesticulation that they would like a lift further down the road. Given all their efforts this was the least we could have done however I refused to give them a ride, thinking the inside of the Transit would just become covered in mud, something I have regretted to this day. How thoughtless of me, did it matter? Back in the vehicles we made our way on to Nakuru.

We stopped along the way to Nakuru at a garage, it was a car dealership as I remember with a maintenance area. Sand and grit had got into the Transit's clutch and I was finding it increasingly hard to change gear. The garage had a look and put a pile of grease on the clutch but said I should take it in to the Ford dealer when we reached Nairobi, who would have the necessary spare parts.

Nakuru itself had a small airport and it had become a municipality in 1952, having been a township previously. However as time was pressing we just drove through without stopping, just noticing there were very many brick built properties around, the first we had seen in quite some time. Out of interest Nakuru is in fact today the fourth largest city in Kenya after Nairobi, Mombasa and Kisumu.

From Nakuru we drove along much improved tarmac roads to Nairobi, quite noticeably a more relaxed driving experience all round. Although the combi was holding its own, the Transit noticeably began 'crabbing' in that the back was out of alignment with the front. We pulled over and I crawled underneath the vehicle to have a look, only to find with despair I might add, that the front axle was bent! We could not do a thing about it there and then so we decided to just keep on driving. When we reached Nairobi later that day we found somewhere to stay. Coming into the town we noticed a Church on the way in, a Scottish Presbyterian Church as it happened and we drove through the main gates and stopped. We walked around to see if there was anyone about. At this point the American with us decided to leave for the airport to organise his flight home. We thanked him for driving the combi said our goodbyes and he took off anxious to get back home. Fortunately the church warden was on the premises. We told him about our situation and he said we could camp out on their grassed lawn. He gave us a key for their toilet and shower annex which was attached to the Church, this was a joy and a delight after weeks of being the great unwashed. We had not realised at this point that in actual fact the Nairobi authorities had a camp site on the outskirts of the city. Having set up camp we then walked into the town to the Ford dealers repair centre who said it would cost us the equivalent of £17.50 to replace the clutch on the Transit, the front axle being far too expensive to even contemplate repairing. We decided we would just manage the crabbing issues and took the Transit in to them.

Out of interest Menai and myself took the Transit to the new Ford showroom and asked whether they would be interested in displaying the Transit, given it had travelled all the way from London to Nairobi. The manager, who was British said yes much to our amazement and said they would pay us to exhibit it. We left the Transit there for about four days as we did not need it. When we returned, the manager, who had previously been so enthusiastic was suddenly totally disinterested. For no clear reason he gave us the keys, asked us to take it away, no mention of payment discussed. Another lesson learned re ex pats as we were to witness later on.

# Chapter Thirteen

Whilst we were in Nairobi I also purchased a rifle, everyone seemed to have one it seemed a necessity. On the road to Ethiopia we had met up with another English couple on route. 'Have you not got a gun?' the English man asked me, 'you really need one for protection!' They said they had been glad of their rifle on a couple of occasions, to frighten local natives off. To be honest I had not given this any thought but now the thought was in my mind, I decided perhaps this was something we needed to have although I did not think for a second I could ever shoot anything or anyone with one. Someone directed us to a store called 'The Bunduki'. Every hunting weapon you could wish for was on display in this place. I had a good look around and as you might expect was harassed into purchasing something which was completely out of my price range and most definitely unnecessary for a simple traveller. Eventually I left and went to another local dealer, tried to negotiate over a rifle and was obviously and completely out of my depth. The dealer informed me that his prices were at least a third less than the Bunduki and he was therefore not open to any negotiation and so I acquiesced and bought a rifle from him, with some ammunition which I hoped I would never have to use.

Whilst in camp, I kept five rounds in the magazine of the rifle and slept with it at the side of me. One night at camp we heard a noise, knowing there were thieves around as we had been warned. I got up, grabbed the gun and shouted out 'I have a gun here!' I quickly unzipped the tent and leapt out with the rifle, like some poor man's Indiana Jones! As I leapt out I saw three men running away down the grassed lawn at the back of the Church.

The caretaker at the church was allegedly a witch doctor we had been told and on arrival he had locked our suitcases away in the crypt of the Church. Later when we went to the suitcases for a change of clothes, we found the cases had been forced open and all sorts of things stolen, in fact one day we were driving through Nairobi and Menai noticed a woman walking down the street wearing one of her dresses! She knew it was hers as she had made it herself, quite unbelievable.

Whilst camping at the Church, we had also met up with the black Deputy Minister of the Scottish Presbyterian Church who was Kikuyu, he had spent his training years in the US. The actual minister of the Church was in fact Scottish but in our time there we never actually got to meet him for some unknown reason. George, the Deputy lived at the back of the Church with his wife and was I recall very pleasant and very helpful. So Menai and I settled down in camp out of everyone's way. We explored Nairobi not quite sure what we were going to do next as we were very short of money.

As there was just the two of us now we decided we really did not need two vehicles and of the two the combi was the most useful and suitable for carrying on with our journey, so we made the decision to sell the Transit get some money together and press on. During the next days in an attempt to sell the Transit we mixed with some questionable individuals, including the Ford dealers and eventually managed to get a genuine prospective buyer. Several days in Nairobi had passed by now but the prospective buyer, we discovered only had East African shilling to pay us with which essentially was worthless currency as it could not be used outside East Africa. We could have sold it for a good price but it was not to be.

Out of the blue after the tenth day in Nairobi, Nancy and Lou reappeared! Someone had told them we were camping in the Church grounds, word had spread? We met and talked to them and explained what had happened since we saw them last. They said their combi was battered and bruised it's engine in a poor state, in fact they said it was dilapidated. They suggested buying our combi and refitting their own using ours for spare parts and Lou offered us 250 dollars. We thought about it and agreed to this, believing we could manage on that and as time was pressing we decided we had no choice. Lou wanted our combi for parts, ours was a camper and theirs was not and ours had a new engine and steering. 250 dollars at the time equated to about £100.00. Nancy and Lou were staying with a farmer at the time about 20 miles out of Nairobi. The farmer was a well-established Kenyan European farmer with a huge amount of land. Nancy said she would drive our combi back to the farm and they asked us to go up to the farm the following day and meet them there.

The following morning Menai and I travelled up to the farm and found Nancy and Lou in the grounds with the two combis. The farmer Mr. H spoke fluent Kikuyu. He had lived there through the Mau Mau insurrection and explained to us that he had never had any trouble at all with the terrorist group, because essentially it was the Kikuyu fighting off other tribal groups for power, in readiness for when the British gave independence to Kenya. The farmer admitted that the fact he spoke Kikuyu helped considerably with his workers and their tribal leaders and they respected him for this. However one day he had found his pet Alsatian dog pinioned onto metal railings, dead of course. He was incensed and extremely upset as you would imagine, he had thought he would be left alone as his farm was remote. Mr. H told us that he had driven over to the Mau Mau area leaders and confronted them. They had been bemused as to what had taken place but told him that they suspected five of their renegade members who had gone off to start their own group had been responsible and to just leave it to them.

A few days later a message was passed to Mr. H to say that the five renegades had been found and the matter 'resolved,' which he understood to mean they had been killed. He told us that after this there had been no more trouble and added that the Europeans allegedly killed by the Mau Mau had sadly been 'in the wrong place at the wrong time?'

Mr. H had said that Nancy and Lou could use his workshop to take all the bits out of our combi and transfer them to their own, adding that he had a mechanic who would help them do this. I remember Menai and myself feeling a bit sorry about it all, as we had become attached to the combi as you do your vehicles, it felt like a wrench, but what could we do. We were invited into the house at the farm and were presented with an extremely moist ginger cake, with cream, by 'Pedro' who appeared to be head cook, bottle washer etc. for the family. Pedro was a Somali and stood and watched as we devoured every mouthful and every mouthful a delight. In fact to this day I remember it being the most delicious cake I have ever eaten and we told him so at the time. He left us with the biggest smile we had ever seen!

Staying at the farm at the same time as Nancy and Lou was an American soldier who had just finished his tour of duty in Vietnam, a soldier from the Marine Corp. He had been befriended by Mr H's son. The marine was apparently making his way back to the US hitchhiking. Nancy and Lou suggested to us that he join us on our journey, although the marine only had fifty dollars to his name. We were told that Mr. H's grandson had recently and accidentally been killed just days before our arrival though exactly how we never knew. In his grief and for whatever reason Mr H's son offered money to the marine for his journey back to the US and the marine I remember was very emotional about the whole situation. The fact that Mr. H's son who had become a friend would help him out even though he was in such a state of distress himself reduced the marine to tears. After a stressful day it was eventually agreed he would travel on with Menai and myself.

# Chapter Fourteen

For several days I had been getting soreness around my coccyx area, I had not bothered about it initially, but steadily it had become worse. Menai had a look at it and said there was a big red lump there which obviously needed some attention. At the Church we asked George the clergyman, whether he knew of any doctor we could see. George referred us to a particular doctor and we went off to see him, the doctor was a European, an ex-Army medic who diagnosed 'jeep driver's bum!' and said I had a boil in reverse which would need removing as it could become quite dangerous and could grow inwards. Fortunately Menai and I had insurance and fortuitously the insurance company had an office in Nairobi so we went to see them, they agreed to foot the bill for the operation and the doctor booked me into the hospital. A Mr Green did the operation under general anaesthetic at a total cost of £1,500. They kept me in for a few days and I was discharged back to our campsite with a box of dressings as I recall. Whilst I was in hospital Menai stayed with one of the hospital administrators who she had befriended, as she understandably did not want to stay at the campsite alone.

After the operation Menai and I slept at George's house at the Church at his invitation, his wife was pregnant at the time. George I remember was what you would call a thoroughly nice man. Although he had a car George was still learning to drive and I said to him that I would drive his wife to hospital when she was ready to have the baby as she was almost due. A few days later George came to us and said Mary his wife was ready to go to hospital and I said that was no problem at all. Mary was a lovely woman at least six foot tall and towered over me, George too for that matter. Mary said she could have had the baby the previous night, but she had not wanted to disturb me! She said she had held it in, what can you say?? I took her very swiftly to the hospital which was about ten miles away and remember on the journey there she was so calm you would never have believed it, given she was about to have a baby! I think I was panicking for them both. I dropped George and Mary off in the nick of time and before long they were proud owners of a baby girl. All was well.

When I returned to the campsite at the back of the Church, the Scottish lads from earlier on our journey reappeared. Someone had told them that we were camping there so they stopped by to say hello, still full of the joys of travelling and full of optimism, despite the fact that one of them had contracted venereal disease in Ethiopia! He told us he had had some medication for it and that it had cleared up, he seemed none the worse for his experience. Otherwise the lads were unscathed and anxious to move on again and off they went. We were glad to have caught up with them fellow travellers in a strange land.

I went back to see the surgeon in Nairobi and he advised me to bathe in the salt water sea of Mombasa to speed up the healing following my operation, it was agreed that we could achieve nothing more in Nairobi and Menai and I said our goodbyes to George the clergyman and his wife, which was quite emotional given all that happened to all of us in such a short space of time. We were genuinely sad to leave them. We said our goodbyes to the warden also and then to Nancy and Lou once again and packed up with our new passenger on board to set off for Mombasa, the second largest city after Nairobi and a history full of Swahili traditions. Historically of course Vasco de Gama had been the first known European to visit Mombasa, although as I have read, not with the greatest reception at the time from the local tribesmen!

Having said our goodbyes to Nancy and Lou they had a sudden change of mind and decided that in fact they would like to join us in Mombasa. All agreed we left together, them in the updated combi and us in the Transit. We set off again along the tarmac road a day's journey to a campsite in Mombasa where we parked under the shelter of palm trees. I was a little apprehensive about swimming in the sea as directed by the surgeon but once we settled in the campsite I took myself off and dipped myself into the salt water at least half a dozen times, which I remember stung like fury but I did as instructed and my wound began to dry up and heal, definitely worth the suffering! Salt water obviously the way forward.

The campsite in Mombasa had lots of millipedes as I recall and we had to make sure we cleared them out of the tent. The campsite actually belonged to a hotel and between the hotel and the campsite was a snack/coffee bar. After a day or two we called into the coffee bar and there was no one else there other than ourselves and another white lady. We went over and said hello and she came and sat with us all, Menai, myself, Nancy, Lou and the marine. She told us her name was Lady Isabel, wife of Sir Charles, who had been governor of Sudan many years before and they had retired to what was then Rhodesia. This was the period when Rhodesia had declared UDI from Britain, i.e. just wanting a 'white' Government and Robert Mugabe was leader of the terrorists/freedom fighters.

Lady Isabel had come up the coast for a short break on a cruise ship which she said she was picking up again a few days later. She was staying at the hotel on her own and took quite a shine to our marine and said she would see if she could help him find some work when he arrived in Rhodesia. We spent three days in Mombasa and over the days we saw her every day, we seemed to be the only tourists there.

On the last day Lady Isabel took a taxi back to her cruise ship. We said goodbye to Nancy and Lou who were returning to Mr H's farm. This time it was a proper goodbye but for some reason we never exchanged addresses or promised to keep in touch even though we had formed quite a friendship by then? We just wished each other well and looking back perhaps a little effort on both our parts should have been made. Another of those inadequate partings of the ways.

That day we also left the campsite in Mombasa and drove on South. After about three hours we arrived at the Tanzania border where the border guards made a big fuss about our passports but we were allowed through thankfully. On the other side of the border we stopped for a coffee and took out a flask we had bought in Nairobi only to find it was broken and I remember hoping it was not a bad omen, no coffee no caffeine to keep us going sadly. On route through Tanzania we noted a lot of Chinese workers on the backs of trucks all wearing coolie hats. We were told later that The Peoples Republic of China were extending the railway system in East Africa at the time and only employed their own Chinese labour. The Chinese Government's expectation was that these workers would not return to China, they would become residents of Tanzania and that was why we had seen so many trucks full of Chinese driving about on these roads. We continued our journey on the

Serengeti Plain which was very flat with hills in the distance, vast expanses of golden sand with the odd shrub dotted here and there. It was hot, dusty and Mount Kilimanjaro was somewhere about. All we could think about was the lure of a good cup of coffee as we sped along the graded dirt roads.

We eventually came to a Roman Catholic mission where we stayed the night and in fact we ended up staying at several others whilst we travelled through Tanzania. The missions were always friendly and welcoming, free of course and we believed the priests loved to see new faces given most of them had spent a lifetime living in those missions and new faces most probably few and far between.

It was in the Southern Serengeti we suddenly noticed a wheel rolling past us speeding it's away into the grassland. Suddenly the Transit went down on the right hand side with a massive bang! The vehicle stopped and we jumped out only to find one of the rear wheel on the right had come off, the wheel nuts were lost but we did manage to retrieve the wheel at least. It was a hot and cloudy day I remember and we sat there on the dusty road wondering what to do next. Our marine given all that military training no doubt, came up with a bright idea. What we needed to do was to take one nut off of each of the other three wheels and put them back onto the wheel that needed them and then get to a garage as soon as possible. Problem solved and that was exactly what we did, jacked up the Transit, tightened all the nuts and prayed. Whether this was meant to be who knows but as we finished the job we all turned to look behind us and there in the distance clear as day was Mount Kilimanjaro in all its glory, rising majestically through the clouds! It was spectacular sight mystical almost, a view to behold and one we would never ever forget. Mount Kilimanjaro, a dormant volcano, over 19,000 feet above sea level surrounded at it's peak in dazzling whiteness. It was breathtaking, we were speechless.

From there we drove into the town of Arusha, at the base of the volcanic Mount Meru, the Serengeti National Park to its west. Eventually we came across an Asian run garage where we stopped and got out of the vehicles, glad to stretch our legs for a while. We spoke to the mechanics who said that we had no chance of obtaining any spare parts. However they did have a large selection of spare nuts and bolts and said they might do the job and that they would be willing to try and fit them. Thankfully and to our utmost relief they did just that, we were most grateful.

# Chapter Fifteen

To be honest at this point we did very little sightseeing at this time, we just wanted to keep going to achieve our goal. Eventually we drove into Malawi, a landlocked country bordered by Zambia to the North West, Tanzania to the North East and Mozambique, separated from Tanzania and Mozambique by Lake Malawi. Dr. Hastings Banda was President of Malawi at the time, he was in fact an ex- GP from Liverpool who only spoke English so only had English taught in the schools in Malawi.

At the Malawi border we went into the Customs office and we told the officer we had a rifle with us. The Customs officer was quite adamant, 'oh, no,' he said 'you cannot bring that over the border, we will keep it for you until you come back!' I said I would not be coming back and I asked to speak to someone in charge. I was advised I would need to speak to the Police Chief. I asked the Customs officer if I were able to obtain a letter from the Chief of Police allowing me access to Malawi with the rifle, would that be sufficient? He said it would but he still insisted on keeping the rifle. There were no issues with passports or anything else so we left the building minus the rifle.

As we approached the Transit, we noticed a huge group of boys dressed like boy scouts opening the doors of the transit and scrambling about inside like a mound of ants, the door had not been locked. Menai and I asked the boys what they thought they were doing and they said they were doing 'their job?' which allegedly was checking vehicles coming into Malawi. These boys looked only to be about ten to twelve years old, the oldest maybe fifteen! Menai immediately went into 'school teacher mode' and shooed them all out. They were so surprised at being chastised they scrambled out again. I asked the oldest boy who it was that was in charge of them and he said it was a man in the village on the nearby hillside. Very irritated by the whole scenario, Menai and I shut the doors of the Transit, locked up and marched off up the path towards the buildings up on the hillside, with all twenty boys following behind us, dressed in green uniforms with neckerchiefs and oversized boots without laces I might add clomping along. It all seemed very tragic in some ways and me like the Pied Piper.

We eventually got to an office and we walked in and demanded to know who was allowing these young boys to run riot. The man in charge asked the boys to leave and the atmosphere was extremely uncomfortable as I recall. The man we spoke to said he was in charge of the Young Pioneer Corp in the area and I asked him was it normal practice to allow children to behave in such a totally undisciplined manner? Menai said quite vehemently that she thought this was the way children behave when they have no proper leadership or guidance and questioned why they were not in school learning to read and write . The man was clearly embarrassed and so in order to bring some calm to the situation I said to him that the children were welcome to have a look around the Transit in a civilised manner but Menai insisted 'without boots.' Before we returned to the Transit the man selected four boys to come down with us, the doors of the Transit were opened again and we agreed that they could look around in an organised manner and open the suitcases if they wished.

Following the 'inspection' we drove off to search for the Chief of Police's outpost. Our marine appeared not to want to get involved he just kept out of the way mostly and sat around with his own thoughts. Six miles down the dirt road we passed a compound of single storey buildings and we turned in and noticed a large American camping vehicle parked up, a Winnebago to be precise. We got out and walked over to the vehicle and a couple appeared. He was a retired police chief from Ohio, it transpired and we said hello and had a chat about our situation and he said 'I bet the first thing you want is a cold beer!' He was right of course, but we needed to find the Police chief first. We left our marine with the Winnebago couple to indulge himself in a beer or two, whilst we went off in search of the office and said we would be back shortly.

We were eventually taken to the Chief and we explained who we were. The Chief of Police was a tall heavily built man, courteous and friendly. We explained in detail what had happened at the border. He asked me what sort of rifle I had in my possession and I said it was a '22,' 'that would not kill an ant!' he said and asked where we were from. I said we were from Manchester. 'Oh,' he said, 'I know the Town Hall and the Library!' Menai and I were bemused until he explained that he had been to Hutton Police College near Preston, which we knew of, most unexpected and surprising. The Chief continued to talk to us in a 'gentle way' there was no aggression in his tone at all and we talked about Manchester itself in some depth.

Following our 'chat' the chief picked up a couple of sheets of paper from his clerk and kindly wrote his letter of permission for us by hand and then stamped it, such was our relief. He said that the border control should not give us any trouble now and on our return he said we could stay the night at the Police headquarters if we needed. Menai and myself shook his hand and returned to the Winnebago and settled down for a couple of well deserved and very cool lagers which even now I remember tasted like nectar, straight out of their state of the art fridge ! The couple told us that they had actually broken down and they were waiting for a local man to fit a new piston. After a long pleasant chat with the couple, we all returned to the Transit and went back to the customs office and gave them the letter. The customs officer was clearly very happy that his back was covered and handed me the rifle. We drove back to the Police post and set up camp for the night.

The following night we stayed at a monastery which we just happened to pass on route. On spec we just knocked on the door and suddenly a monk appeared. He looked us over as we asked him politely if we could camp outside. He spoke some English which we were grateful for and he said he could offer us a room, thinking there were just two men. When we explained we had a lady with us he could not deal with this and so we camped on the grass at the front of the monastery. The monks let us use their toilet facilities such as they were. The cloisters I remember were made of privet hedge and some of the monks were walking around the grounds focussed on their breviaries.

As we left the monastery the following day the Transit's battery light began flickering. We made our way to the nearest big town Lilongwe and found a Ford dealer who had no spare parts. They took the alternator off, cleaned it of dust and debris, put it back and it seemed okay. The warning light had gone off and so we carried on to Zomba where we picked up some letters from home from the British Embassy. We had asked relatives to write to us there as there was very little chance of picking up any mail elsewhere. Of course in those days without email, mobile phones etc. any communication was sporadic but always welcome and letters were all we had.   After we picked up our letters we continued on our journey.   Doing all the driving myself was never a problem and as the marine was not insured, Menai and the marine just sat in the back taking in the sights.

# Chapter Sixteen

The following night we camped out in another Roman Catholic mission and then up at first light we made our way the following morning to the Mozambique border which at that time was still a Portuguese colony. The immigration officers let us through with no trouble at all thankfully. The town itself was full of Portuguese soldiers and we did question why they were not fighting the insurgency out of town. We were told later that most of the soldiers were conscripts who were doing National Service and much preferred to be in town. Outside the towns most places were allegedly lawless and we were warned by the Army that the road that would take us to what was then Rhodesia was 'mined' by insurgents!' All we could think at the time was how on earth would we see the mines which of course would be buried? We were apprehensive as you would imagine, but we had no choice. We made our way out of town onto the dirt road and as we travelled down the road we saw many vehicles lying on their sides at the edge of the road obviously having ran over these mines, explosively damaged and oil splattered everywhere. Our hearts were literally in our mouths as we crawled slowly along the road and fortunately with the grace of God we evaded any mines. A miracle in our eyes!

After some time and an element of calm restored we arrived alongside the Zambesi River. At the time there was no bridge in situ to cross the river, for us the only option was a pontoon. The river itself was three miles wide at this point and we were towed across the river on the pontoon by a powerful tug. The master of the tug had a certain technique for towing the pontoon across. I remember there being no rails at all on the pontoon we were just dragged off the shoreline and pulled scarily across the river to the other side where the pontoon was swung around to be grounded on the opposite shoreline. Menai and I were hanging onto the Transit to make sure we did not fall off and the relief of arriving on the other side safely was beyond words.

Off we set again with nowhere to stay and no knowledge of where we might stop the night but we could see streetlights in the distance and we just headed straight for them. We came across a small community of bungalows with Portuguese families living in them and we drove into the middle of these bungalows to a small square and knocked on one of the doors and asked to speak to someone. They spoke no English but took us to the leader of the community who did speak some English. He was very friendly and said we could stay in the community guest house. Initially we were very thankful to have somewhere to stay the night but in fact the place was filthy and full of bugs floor to ceiling, despite having a cold shower and a toilet. We thanked the leader not wanting to offend him in any way but we thought we would take our chances and sleep in the Transit instead and make the best of it. Our American friend said he would take his chances in the guest house, I remember him saying he had 'seen enough bugs in Vietnam to last him a lifetime! The fields around the community had a plague of mili bugs, being nocturnal creatures they all came out at night, crawling up your trousers if you could not catch them fast enough ! Menai and I settled down in the Transit, the streetlights went out at 9.00 p.m. There was a generator on site that went off at that time.

At daybreak we went over to check on our marine all the mili bugs having retreated to the fields of maize by then. He seemed to have survived the night. There was a bottle gas stove in the bungalow and so we boiled some water and had our first instant coffee for what seemed like an age. It was very welcome and I remember we breakfasted on some stale bread and extremely soft (as you would imagine in that heat) butter and marmalade, making do as always.

We went off that morning to thank the community leader for allowing us to stay and he gave us directions to the Rhodesian border.

# Chapter Seventeen

It was an uneventful drive to the Mozambique border with Rhodesia and we passed through without any difficulties. On the Rhodesian side, now in Ian Smith's Rhodesia, he of UDI fame (Unilateral Declaration of Dependence), the Immigration officers were black and the Customs officers white. The Immigration officers were happy to let Menai and myself through however they were not happy to let our marine in as he did not have enough money? All seemed extremely disorganised and the Customs officer looked on hopelessly. I suggested to the Immigration officers that I give our friend the money he required and I asked whether they would then be prepared to let him in. They said yes 'that would be in order' so that is what I did and as soon as we were on our way again, our friend returned the cash to me. Words failed us.

Back on the dirt road we carried on with our journey and came across a roadside café which was quite unexpected and which was run by a black couple. We parked up and had a chilled Coca Cola the first in a long time. It was a hot, sunny day and that cold dark nectar was very welcome. After quenching our thirst we continued to drive along a tarmac road which took us all the way to Bulawayo. We stopped for one night there and camped on a proper site with washing and toilet facilities.

The following morning we carried on to Salisbury. At the border post we had changed some money for Rhodesian pounds and been given petrol coupons as fuel was rationed at the time due to the world embargo against Rhodesia. Outside Bulawayo we filled up using the coupons. Closer to Salisbury, we were aware of a 'siege mentality.' At the time Robert Mugabe's terrorist/freedom fighters were scattered in the area. There were patrols on the roads and people walking around with pistols and rifles over their shoulders. The atmosphere felt quite uncomfortable and unsettling. However we stayed in an organised campsite that night and decided we would call in on Lady Isabel from earlier in our travels. We had her address though we had never thought we would have reason to call on her during our time in Mombasa.

On arrival at her address we drove up to a strikingly palatial house, with obligatory tennis court and parked up at the front door. Quite over awed by the property we rang the doorbell and a black maid came to the door. We asked to speak to Lady Isabel who suddenly appeared like a vision from around the side of the house. It was immediately clear by the look on her face that she was not at all pleased to see us. In fact her manner was so completely different from the affable and gregarious woman we had befriended earlier in our travels? She asked us what we were doing at her house and we explained about what had happened and that we had thought to call as we were in the area and still had her address. Lady Isabel reluctantly, or so we believed, invited us into her home and said we should stay for a meal, where things did improve slightly in conversational terms.

In the meantime I asked if I could have a walk around the grounds and stretch my legs etc. As I was walking about I came across a gentleman sat in a chair quite a distance from the house. It transpired he was in fact Sir Charles who was extremely pleasant and charming and sadly not there when we ate later. We wondered if there was a rift between them? It seemed odd. The meal that followed I remember was excellent, the food delicious and served to us by black servants all dressed in white with white caps. However Lady Isabel reprimanded the staff embarrassingly during the meal, annoyed they were serving the meal from the wrong direction etc. etc. which from our point of view was highly unnecessary. We felt extremely sorry for them but quite unable to intervene as guests. Lady Isabel asked us where we were staying and we said we were staying at a local campsite and she asked us whether we would prefer to stay at her home overnight as opposed to returning to the site, which we thought was very considerate given the circumstances. She offered a room to Menai and said our marine and myself could sleep in the garage, which is what we did.

The next day we had breakfast and then drove back to the campsite. Lady Isabel had been chatting to our marine the previous evening asking him what he was going to do next. She had apparently spoken to someone following their conversation, a friend who had a tourist ranch. Their son (in his 30's) had recently died. We never knew the circumstances but obviously the family were still grieving. They were missing their son and quite obviously struggling to manage the ranch without him and as we understood they had very few staff. To cut a long story short the couple came to the campsite to talk to our marine and eventually it was decided that he would return to their ranch with them to help them out. He told Menai and I that he would hang around for a while to see what he could do there. We wondered whether the couple might perceive him as a surrogate son which seemed so sad and maybe not the real answer but it was his decision . We said our goodbyes reluctantly knowing we would miss his friendly banter, his accent and his answers for everything! Packed up and ready, Menai and I travelled on south.

# Chapter Eighteen

The two of us made our way down south to Beit Bridge which was the South African border. We had no other focus than to keep on travelling now. We just needed to keep on going. Motivation at this point after such a long and stressful journey had been lost along the way. We had a destination and that was as far as our thoughts took us. We were very tired and weary and arrived at the border post and parked up . These were the days of the so called 'wonderfully white days of apartheid.' The South African customs gave us no trouble checked out the rifle again with just a bit of advice to go to the local Magistrate for a certificate once we were settled.

Rightly or wrongly, Menai and I felt as though we had finally reached 'civilisation' as we knew it. Suddenly we were driving on dual carriageways, something we could relate to. There were parks and gardens and all that

Europe had in common, everything organised and planned out. Initially we had no awareness of the apartheid system, to us it was almost like being at home. Friends and relatives thought we were stupid and foolish to even undertake such a project and with hindsight we knew we had been naïve and unprepared. Personally I had a point to prove. Having started the ball rolling pride would not allow any turning back however haphazard the journey or plans. To actually reach South Africa had been an achievement, something I had not experienced before.

The first night in Beit Bridge we camped out at a Local Authority campsite which was to be fair very clean and tidy, a public campsite. The Transit by some miracle was still driveable, still 'crabbing' but still in one piece. The climate had not changed it was still very hot and very humid. We made our way to Mafeking the next day where Baden Powell had been General during the Boer War. We stayed in the grounds of the local Methodist Church and the following morning the minister of the church took us to the office of the Mafeking Mail newspaper. At great length they wrote about our story which appeared in print a few days later! (our fifteen minutes of fame perhaps?) When we had finally settled in Durban we contacted the Mail office to ask them whether we could have a copy of the newspaper and were astounded that we had been 'headline news! The most exciting thing that had happened that week. Mafeking itself was an interesting town and still unbelievably had hitching posts for horses just like you would see in the old cowboy films.

After that little bit of excitement Menai and I travelled to Johannesburg a cosmopolitan city high up in the Transvaal with European type weather, cool winters, warm summers - that sort of thing. We camped in the Johannesburg suburb of Krugersdorp and whilst we were there took the opportunity of visiting an acquaintance we had met a long time previously in London. Tony was a schoolteacher who lived in Krugersdorp with his mother and father. Menai had written to say we would call if we could but at the time we had no idea when or if that might be. Tony was pleased to see us and absolutely amazed that we had managed to get there! He tried to persuade Menai to stay there and find work, but there were few opportunities around at the time and she had of course already secured a post in Durban. We were very short of money at the time and for us gaining income had to be the priority. Tony showed us around the suburb where the apartheid system became quite obvious; doorways to almost everywhere segregated, doorways for blacks, and doorways for whites. It was quite unbelieveable.

After our visit we continued on our journey to our final destination after nine long and eventful months and some very hair raising and stressful moments. In the gestation time of a baby we had experienced every emotion imaginable, four hundred miles and twelve hours later we had arrived. Durban was like a European city and we felt quite at home from the start though strangely there was no sense of excitement, just relief mostly. We had no plan other than to get ourselves settled in as soon as possible and start earning some money. For a day or two we stayed in a trailer park and then got some lodgings for several days with an objectionable woman who took umbrage that we were not staying for a lengthy period of time. In fact she even refused to let us cook or do our washing on our final day before we moved to an apartment on West Street in Durban which would be our home for the next four years. That day another new adventure about to begin.

Just a short while after we had settled in Durban we received a letter from the Chairman of the renowned Bank mentioned previously in our travels advising us that we owed £32.00 for the famous carnet de passages! We had no idea how the son of the Chairman, one of our group had managed to locate us, but in between times we had run into two of our fellow travellers the solicitor and the ex-postmistress who had since settled together in Durban, following their escape to Nairobi. Menai and I wondered whether they were in contact with his son and had told him of our whereabouts. It was some days later that his son motorcycled over from Rhodesia, where he had settled himself, to tell us that we owed his father, the Chairman £32.00 for the carnet de passages. It was obviously a huge issue for him and the fact that he had motor cycled that distance and gone to the trouble of finding us spoke volumes! Menai and I had no intention of not paying what we owed them and as requested we settled this straight away at the local Post Office and paid his father in £1.00 postal orders as I recall. Everyone happy.

It seemed both strange and a little sad to Menai and I that after so many months of living so closely with such a small group of people, that essentially we only ever had a superficial understanding of one another knowing each other intimately at times it seemed but not in reality. Individually we were all on some sort of a mission, for each of us that meant something very different. From our own perspective we felt that at the end of the journey, given all we had been through together as a group, that firm friends or at least some connection ought to have been made. The reality being we had all just drifted away from each other and moved on with apparent ease. Relationships had been challenging at times as some relationships are yet it seemed the solicitor and the ex-postmistress had found a little pocket of happiness in all that chaos, obviously meant to be and a positive!

One of the most 'stand out' memories of the improved tarmac roads of South Africa along our journey, were the rows of Jacaranda trees lining several routes resplendent and full of vibrant purple blue blossoms, a welcome sight after many challenging dirt tracks and very little else apart from bush land. Apparently jacarandas are not indigenous to South Africa and were introduced from Brazil to South Africa in 1829 but I remember they were indeed a sight to behold. It seemed as if we were being drawn along the highways by these wonderful trees and all they had to offer. A wonderful view, a treat for the eyes and just one of those special memories.

As for the famous Transit the chariot of steel that had survived all manner of problems en route and had delivered us in one piece, we knew the front axle was bent and we had paid £850.00 for it new.

Once we had settled into our apartment in Durban we decided it was time to let the Transit go as it was far too big for us, not what we needed from that point onwards. We advertised in the local newspaper and were absolutely amazed at the demand for it. The first people we talked to were a group of mixed race men who told us they were only able to buy with hire purchase from a finance company and the finance company were insisting the front axle was straightened before they released the money. We felt very mean at the time but we thought this was a lot of hassle and just wanted to sell it soon and free up some cash. Eventually we ended up selling the Transit to an Afrikaans farmer who had driven 300 miles from Cape Province. He needed it as he had a contract with the Local Authority to do the school run.

When we met the farmer and his brother, their conversation centred solely on justifying apartheid, a subject we really did not want to get involved with so we just sat and listened and said very little at all. As for the Transit he said he would do the necessary repairs himself and offered us 1000 rand, which was approximately

£500.00. We agreed the figure shook hands on it and he drove off in the Transit, with his brother trailing behind in their vehicle. We had to pay 100 rand import duty before he could re-register the Transit as it still had British number plates, but he trusted us to do this after he left and we promised to let him know when this had been done. After such an incredible journey, as with the combi, we had grown very attached to the Transit and it was with heavy heart we let that go too. It was an emotional time for us both. Eight wheels and a prayer we had got there in the end.

# ROUTE MAP
'Map courtesy of Theodora.com/maps used with permission'

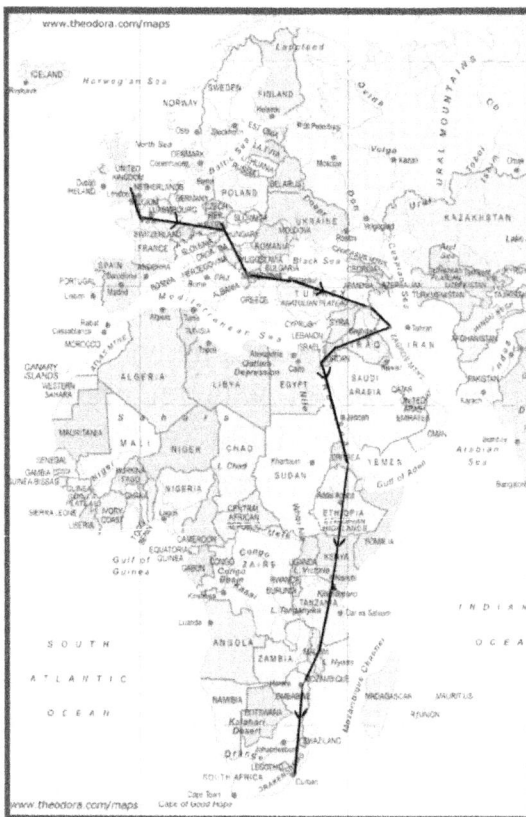

What we could do with hindsight we can all say that. All 'ideas' seem like a good idea at the time. We or should I say I had an idea not a project a need to escape and to do 'something different.' We all learned lessons as you do, life just being one long teaching session it seems. We met some very interesting people along the way and were glad to have had all those relationships albeit temporarily and those experiences which today are cause for thoughtful recollection.

Menai sadly died several years ago, but I know if she were here today she would say 'it was an adventure every day' and it was.

Accepting your mistakes, not blaming others for your lack of luck, not feeling frustrated by your failures and remembering that the teachings of your past will always enhance your future is paramount. Wake up to the sun and sleep with the moon and know that you achieved something that day.

CONTACT
john.keeble3@hotmail.co.uk

Copyright John Keeble 2018

Printed in Great Britain
by Amazon

21038384R00099